PRAISE FOR *Climbing Home*

"All of us are interested in getting home one way or another, but the journey is often confusing and difficult. In *Climbing Home*, Madoc Thomas is just the right mix of truth-telling realist, visionary prophet, and gentle-but-firm trail guide. In these pages, you will find the answers of how to negotiate the steep grades of virtues and the stark cliffs of your spiritual questions while engaging in the essential companionship of one who is climbing with us. Read slowly and carefully, but start climbing."

TERRY HARGRAVE, PHD, BESTSELLING AUTHOR
PROFESSOR OF MARRIAGE AND FAMILY THERAPY,
FULLER THEOLOGICAL SEMINARY

"In *Climbing Home*, Madoc Thomas delicately blends the wisdom of a psychotherapist with the authenticity of a believer who has found his way home. This book will challenge you to look at the valleys in your life as simply stops along the path to becoming healthy, whole, and complete in Christ. No matter what stage you may be on your journey of life, you too can find your way home.

DEBRA FILETA, MA, LICENSED PROFESSIONAL COUNSELOR
AUTHOR OF *TRUE LOVE DATES*

"*Climbing Home* represents a lifetime's search for wisdom, enriched by personal and counseling experience. The result is an eminently readable book supported by careful theological underpinnings—truly a remarkable achievement that will enrich Christian readers' understanding of pain in the valley or joy on the mountain of life's faith journey. Read it with highlighter in hand; you likely will want to revisit this one frequently."

BETH PRATT, FORMER RELIGION EDITOR FOR TWENTY-FIVE YEARS WITH
THE LUBBOCK AVALANCHE-JOURNAL.

"Madoc Thomas has written this significant book for all of us who live in this broken world and thus are fighting a variety of battles. Thomas writes from the midst of the fray, having fought many of his own battles. But the chief point of the book is not about wounds and combat, but about grace—the reality that because grace became flesh in Jesus Christ, you and I need never fight any battle alone. That's Good News. Take up and read...and be blessed."

Rev. Ron Scates, former senior pastor
Highland Park Presbyterian Church, Dallas, TX

"*Climbing Home* is a real book, written by a real person, who lives in the real circumstances of life and offers hope that all events of life can lead to something better. Overcoming obstacles prepares us for the greater view of how life can be. It emphasizes real experiences and real possibilities. It offers the "rocks" that former climbers have left that can be helpful to us. But the ultimate climb home is a personal adventure. You will be challenged, inspired, and motivated by Madoc Thomas' treatment of life as we all experience it—and how we *can* experience it!"

John Ed Mathison, nationally known speaker
founder of John Ed Mathison Leadership Ministries
author of seven books, including *When God Redefines the Possible*

"We have known Madoc for over twenty years, and through his own experience, life work, and challenges, he has been a great coach, mentor, and friend. His wisdom comes directly from the Holy Spirit and can lead to a discovery of our true identities in Christ as individuals, couples, and families. We encourage you to read *Climbing Home*, knowing that it is from the heart of a true follower of Christ."

Todd E. Holt, CFP, and Amy Holt, marketing director
Austin, TX

"I am pleased, after knowing Madoc Thomas for over twenty years as a gifted theologian, therapist, teacher, supervisor, minister, and family man, that he is sharing his Christian walk and work in *Climbing Home.* Madoc describes the heavenly places where God gives each of us harmony with him, each other, and nature. If we pay attention to God's whispers through this book, God will take us from our daily struggles into that surreal place where we have a glimpse of heaven on earth."

SUZANNE FOLEY, LICENSED PROFESSIONAL COUNSELOR
LICENSED MARRIAGE AND FAMILY THERAPIST, LUBBOCK, TX

"If you can own and embrace the fact that you are a human struggler, you will find this book very illuminating. Dr. Thomas, a wise and human struggler himself, challenges the reader to grapple with fundamental questions about faith, hope, and love. When troubles come, the reader will be left with the foundational belief that they can indeed "climb home."

ANN NOBLE, PHD, LICENSED MARRIAGE AND FAMILY THERAPIST
LUBBOCK, TX

"God has used *Climbing Home* to show me that I can find pleasure and happiness in a fallen world, and I can find glimpses of heaven here on earth. In these pages you will find prophetic wisdom pointing you to Jesus Christ and His grace. I know Madoc Thomas' words will bless many as they have blessed me."

EMILY SCATES, ASSOCIATE MINISTER OF CHILDREN'S MINISTRY
HIGHLAND PARK PRESBYTERIAN CHURCH, DALLAS, TX

"*Climbing Home* is like a guidebook for the Christian life with another traveler's notes written inside! This is a valuable tool for individuals, families, and groups who want to explore the journey of faith."

LENAE MOORE, LICENSED PROFESSIONAL COUNSELOR
DALLAS, TX

"*Climbing Home* is practical, easy to understand and apply, and offers a positive word of hope that God is bringing us into an unbelievably full life, even when his presence may at times be barely evident. I enthusiastically point readers to this book."

CHUCK WILLIAMS, AUTHOR OF *ETERNAL ROUTE 66*
PLANO, TX

"Madoc Thomas has written a touching book, demonstrating how Christ not only shares in the joy of our good times but is teaching and leading us, step by step, through our obstacles and pain. The chapters on hope and pain were particularly meaningful for me after the recent loss of a child. Those chapters, the suggested Scriptures, and the questions at the end of each chapter helped me find healing, a measure of peace, and hope. Written with gentle simplicity and great depth, this is a book that will be read and reread by many."

Toni Christian, MEd, Licensed Professional Counselor

"*Climbing Home* embraces the reality that all of us, at one point or another, struggle with and question ourselves—and even Jesus Christ. Dr. Thomas guides readers through fundamental questions to help us emerge from despair and begin a journey toward the heavenly places in our earthly lives. This book instills hope that, regardless of how shadowy the valley may seem, we can find immense strength in living a life deeply rooted in Christ's love."

Rachael Ward, MEd, licensed professional counselor candidate
Denver, CO

"How many times has God placed someone in your path to direct your climb, with wisdom in the grand adventure of growth in Christ? God can use *Climbing Home* to speak to you wherever you are on this path. Each page encourages the reader to reach for the summit of joy in Christ and all that God has for us here on earth."

Kristi Abbot
Midland, TX.

"My friend, Madoc Thomas, shows believers how Jesus Christ has been with him and can be with us in all life situations."

William L. Deal, retired businessman
Georgetown, TX

Climbing Home

CLIMBING HOME

From Valleys of Despair to Mountains of Hope

E. Madoc Thomas

Climbing Home

Published by
Deep River Books
Sisters, Oregon
www.deepriverbooks.com

ISBN: 9781940269474
Library of Congress: 201410877

Printed in the USA

Cover design by Jason Enterline

To
Calder
Soli Deo Gloria

CAIRNS

Cairns are rocks left by previous climbers to mark a path. They are like the markers God provides which say, “This is the way; walk in it” (Isa. 30:21). They do not stand alone; they stand beside a trail. A cairn is like communion bread, baptismal water, like a hymn, a church bell, a pleasant sunset, a book, a prayer chair, a flower by a path, or the first light of day. Each marker is a witness that points to Jesus: the way, the truth, and the life.

Contents

Preface

God was gently lifting the sun toward the first light of day. It was cold, crisp, and we could just barely begin to see the emerging shapes and sounds above timberline. My wife and I had wanted to climb Mt. Antero, in central Colorado, for some time, and after two previous attempts, this felt like the day.

We had been climbing for two hours toward the sunrise when we began to talk about some of the climbing lessons of our lives. We talked of ourselves, of our thirty-five year journey through many valleys, toward a few summits. We talked of the promise of hope at the first light of day, the sun rising to caress the path ahead. We talked of the church members, the students, the clients, the members of our family, and friends we had seen take steps on the path toward coming alive, toward heavenly places in Christ. We talked of recovery, of struggle, of the failures, the glories, tragedy, and the miracles of Jesus' becoming incarnate in the earthly walk of those we've known and served. And in that first light of day this book began to arrange its shape in our words.

Climbing Home was conceived.

We also lost the trail! The talus we were climbing had become a jumble of rock, strewn about as if by the hand of a giant child playing "throw the boulder." Our headlamps and the dim first light of day just weren't adequate to show the way forward. But then we saw a cairn. A cairn is a familiar and welcome sight to climbers and backpackers. It's basically a pyramid arrangement of rock that shows the way. Even in the dim, half-light of early sunrise, we could see the way, the way to the summit.

Many books about life in Christ fall short of presenting the loss of the trail, the struggle, and at the same time the hope of real life. We and others living in Christ need support in finding the cairns, the markers that point the way at first light, when the trail and the summit are unclear.

This is a book about the path finding, the process of growth out of darkness toward the heavenly fullness of God's light. *Climbing Home* is a word of hope that God is bringing us into the folds of his love even when the shape of his presence is only dimly discerned. It is a book about the journey to the heavenly places in our earthly life.

Climbing Home does not address everyone or everything. It is specifically offered to Christian people who have struggled with life difficulties, questions, and answers that don't work. It is designed for and has grown out of ministry in church, teaching, and counseling to folks in such difficulties as grief, divorce, addiction, depression, and the needs people have for purpose, hope, love, and forgiveness. Another book at another time will perhaps reflect my ministry also to non-Christian and even anti-Christian people.

This book has emerged from many people and many experiences. I thank them all: students, church members, friends, therapists, colleagues, teachers, clients, doctors, ministers, and above all my family, both past and those still present in this earthly life. Special thanks go to many people whose names are not mentioned, but who by a word, a gesture, an encouragement have built cairns with me, have taught me the trail, and have then walked alongside me as we grew up together toward Christ in all things. I am grateful to the wonderful editors, marketing advisors, design team, and other ministers of the written word at Deep River Books, especially publisher Bill Carmichael, associate publisher Andy Carmichael, editorial director Kit Tosello, editor Kathryn Deering, cover designer Jason Enterline, director of author resources Tamara Barnet, and Chris Carmichael, president of Surfperch Communications who was an outstanding help in website design. Several friends and family who were generous with their time, talent, and support contributed significant input into the manuscript and marketing: Kristi Abbott, Toni Christian, William Deal, Debra Fileta, Celeste Flood, Suzanne Foley, Amy Haddock, Dr. Terry Hargrave, Todd and Amy Holt, Dr. John Ed Mathison, Dr. Thomas McGovern, Lenae Moore, Dr. Ann Noble, Beth Pratt, Jo Ann Pointer, Sarah Robertson, Emily Scates, Ron Scates, Calder Thomas, Chris Thomas, Paul Thomas, John Thomas, Rachael Ward, and Chuck Williams. Jesus Christ has above all built the paths, the cairns, and the heavenly places of *Climbing Home,* at and even before the first-light times of our lives, and to him above all, who sits on the summit, all thanks and glory are due.

Introduction

God's children, like all children, have questions. How can I be safe? Will I be alone? Will I have enough of what we need? Where do I belong? What is the truth about the things I care about? Whom can I trust? Are we there yet? How can we see the way, how can we find the trail in the dim half-light of very early morning, when it feels as though we see through a mirror dimly?

Our questions grow out of fundamental needs. We ask about trust because we need reliability to live the truth, not a fantasy or lie. We ask about safety because we need security. We ask about aloneness because God knew our need for relationship was rooted in his own nature, and so said it is not good to be alone (see Genesis 2:18). We ask about purpose because we need to live lives of significance and meaning.

These questions and needs are sometimes represented in the Bible and other Christian literature as the valleys of our lives (see, for example, Psalm 23:4 and Isaiah 40:4). These valleys are sometimes places of trouble, sometimes places of developmental growth, but they are always places where we seek answers to basic life questions and fulfillment of our basic needs. The valleys of our lives are the places from which we begin our journey to the heavenly places of the kingdom of God.

We need and seek out answers, but our answers often fail. In the depths of our valleys we build towers of Babel to attempt to reach the heavenly fulfillments we need. The wealth, power, sex, and defenses we design to meet our needs often leave us empty. We "spend money on what is not bread, and...labor on what does not satisfy" (Isa. 55:2). We are like folks adrift at sea, drinking the saltwater that looks so promising but leaves us thirstier than before and eventually kills us. The failures and frustrated attempts to meet our needs can leave us in a deep despair, a sense that living a good and fulfilled life is a futile effort at best.

We are trying to meet basic needs and to answer the questions common to the people of God. But our sinful predisposition to self-lived life lures us toward answers that either don't work or do us and others harm.

For example, we desperately need relationship, and we discover an answer that doesn't work in promiscuity, gang membership, or other forms of codependency.

So what can we do with these questions, these needs? Is it too simplistic to say that Jesus is the answer to our needs? Or is it that he is the answer but we fail to explore the very earthly ways this answer can enter our hungers, our thirsts, our needs for life and the questions those needs provoke? Jesus is the way, the truth, and the life; he is the answer that breathes into us the breath of life. We are "complete in Him" (Col. 2:10, NKJV); we have abundant, full, and rich life in him (John 10:10); and "the hopes and fears of all the years are met in him."[1] He has promised to meet all our needs, not in a paltry, poor manner but "according to the riches of his glory in Christ Jesus" (Phil. 4:19).

How does Christ actually come alive in us? What happens when the life of Jesus enters the lives of his followers? How do we connect our questions and the Christ? The paths of Christian growth make the connection between our questions and mountains of hope, the heavenly places of life in Christ.

"The heavenly places" is a theme of Paul's letter to the Ephesians. This phrase does not refer to places in heaven but to life on this earth which is lived in the reality of God's heavenly gifts. Paul declares, "God…made us alive together with Christ…and raised us up together, and made us sit together in the heavenly places in Christ Jesus" (Eph. 2:4–6, NKJV). These heavenly places are like the land of Canaan in the Old Testament; they are the realms in which God's life gets worked out in the lives of his people. They are places of hope that our lives can, after all, be good and joyful.

This image of the heavenly places is certainly similar to the views and perceptions of life above timberline to a climber. The issue for climbers, and for us, is how we are to get to the summit, how we are to grow toward the pinnacle of fulfilled needs and answered questions. How can we find the path?

A cairn can help.

Cairns are rocks left by previous climbers to mark a path. They are like the markers God provides which say, "This is the way; walk in it"

(Isa. 30:21). They do not stand alone; they stand beside a trail. A cairn is like communion bread, baptismal water, like the words and tune of a hymn, a church bell, a pleasant sunset, a book, a time of day, a prayer chair, a meal, a flower by a path, or the first light of day. Each of these is a marker, a witness that points to Jesus: the way, the truth, and the life.

The purpose of this book is to describe the valleys, the paths, and the heavenly places I have seen in clients, students, church members, family, and friends as well as in my own life during my seventy-year journey. My wife and I have come alive; we have walked from death to times of heaven on earth and we have seen others do the same. This book is a witness to that work of God in us and in others.

The chapters that follow were written in light of real life experiences. The principles and behaviors, the cairns marking the trails from earthly valleys to heavenly places, have been tested through thirty-five years of ministry. They have worked to give life to me as well as those I have served.

The cairns of *Climbing Home* have not worked because of the author of this book, but because of "the pioneer and perfecter of faith" (Heb. 12:2). We have listened and have become followers of the way, the truth, and the life himself. It was always the verses of his Word, the shadow of his cross, and the presence of his Spirit directing, energizing, and teaching us how and where to walk. Jesus himself was building the markers, giving the experiences that warned of pitfalls. Jesus was the teacher, the wonderful counselor, and the shepherd of our souls, the forerunner who led the way, marked the trail, and walked beside us out of our valleys into the heavenly places.

Our choices to follow Jesus toward the heavenly places of hope revolve around three basic principles: faith, hope, and love. These are the three basic means of receiving, following, and coming alive in Christ. Faith, hope, and love map the contours of the land that leads out of dysfunctional and unsatisfying answers to our needs and questions. These three abide as the stones with which Christ builds the cairns of *Climbing Home*.

The structure of the book intentionally places issues, questions, and needs for love at the central section of *Climbing Home*. There is a dynamic reason for this structure: God's love for us in Jesus Christ, our love for him and ourselves and each other, as well as our love for life in Christ are central in the formation of both our faith and our hope. Love reaches forward into our hearts and draws us into the arms of faith by the Holy Spirit. And that same love is the foundation of our hope; even when we must hope against hope (see Romans 4:18), we can know that nothing can separate us from the power and life-giving influence of God's love (see Romans 8). It is this love of God, creating our salvation and sustaining us in all life's ups and downs, that leads above all out of the valleys of despair up the path of growth toward the heavenly mountains of hope.

The same Lord has built the cairns of faith, hope, and love leading out of numerous valleys of pain and despair; and because the same Lord built these cairns, those leading out of one valley are often similar to those leading out of another. For example, church, strength, and nurture are cairns found in slightly different shapes in several of these chapters. There are also passages of Scripture such as Psalm 23, John 14–16, and Romans 8 which are so multilayered that they appear in many chapters. Jesus Christ is above all the unifying center of each chapter and the experiences which prompted *Climbing Home.* This is above all a word of witness to the one Lord who first climbed home in his resurrection.

Each chapter of the book is divided into four parts:

1. Each is introduced by experiences from real life and ministry. (Identities are carefully altered where these experiences include clients, students, church members, and friends.)
2. *The valleys* include our questions, needs, and unsuccessful attempts to answer those questions and meet those needs.
3. *The paths* toward heavenly places describe the cairns, the markers that have proven most useful in leading us forward.
4. Finally, each chapter paints a picture of what it may look like to live in *the heavenly places.*
5. The conclusion of each chapter includes growth-producing *questions and Scriptures* for further reflection.

God has graciously used my ministry to help many people move out of their valleys and to walk the path to the heavenly places in Christ Jesus. I offer *Climbing Home* with the prayer that you, too, will join me and others whose lives are on the path to the heavenly places in Christ Jesus.

Part I: Questions of Faith

"Where are you from?" It's a common question at initial meetings. A person's origin can reveal a great deal about personality, values, lifestyle, beliefs, and strengths. The people of the first century questioned the validity of Jesus' character when they wondered, "Can any good thing come out of Nazareth?" And I have occasionally seen raised eyebrows when I let someone know I grew up in Birmingham, Alabama.

There are some aspects of our origin we don't choose. We don't choose, as infants, where we're born, who our parents are, the food we eat, sounds we hear, temperature we feel, or even the air we breathe. There are many events throughout our lives over which we have little or no choice. We don't get to choose what season it is or whether we need food, water, and air to live.

But a distinguishing part of human life is our ability to choose largely where we're from in terms of values, attitudes, and beliefs. We can come to life from an attitude of entitlement or we can choose to believe that we are largely responsible for our provisions. We can value pleasure for its own sake or we can see pleasure as interdependent with the needs of others and our commitment to them. We can try to control all our circumstances or we can live with the attitude that we can manage but cannot control all our circumstances.

The origin of our lives, where we're from, is the first part of *Climbing Home*. Each of the first five chapters aims to dispel dysfunctional myths of faith, to indicate some of the cairns that can lead to positive, healthy faith, and describes the heavenly places we can enjoy when we come from the truth of God. The myths include various assaults on faith from the "accuser" of the people of God (Rev. 12:10), as well as claiming to define our lives by the rejection, abuse, or perfectionistic exclusion from God's love by our failures. The way forward includes markers to help us stay on the path, such as worship, devotions, and attachment to people who support our lives in the truth of God. The heavenly places include derivatives of faith such as blessedness or happiness.

These five chapters deal with different dimensions of faith. Identity, for example, is a matter of faith in God's shaping who we are meant to be. Grace deals with life by faith in the unconditional love of God. The goal in these chapters is freedom from origins of life which would impair or destroy us and our growth toward the fulfillment of our lives in Jesus Christ. "Where are you from?" Hopefully, these chapters can empower us to answer, regardless of birthplace, ethnicity, or circumstances, "I am from Jesus Christ."

Chapter 1

TRUTH: Whom can I trust?

Was it really true? On August 13, 2010 it became definite: I had liver cancer. A blood transfusion had led to Hepatitis C, which in turn eventually led to the development of a malignant liver tumor.

I was listed for a liver transplant on September 20, 2010, after innumerable tests to establish my candidacy for that procedure. But there was a subtext to the medical process. Over the weeks and months before the transplant I found myself becoming increasingly positive, hopeful, and joyful even at the prospect of climbing the slopes of this new mountain. I found that what I had said in pulpit and practice, with family and friends, was not only sustaining me, but was filling me with "all joy and peace in believing" (Rom. 15:13, NKJV). After I wrote a letter to clients, family, friends, and colleagues (included in Appendix A), folks began to ask how my wife and I could be so peaceful, so positive. After all, we *were* dealing with the dreaded "C" word, weren't we?

Honestly, I wondered the same thing: "How is this faith happening? Where does this peace come from? Who gave me the hope I experience? Was I in denial?" I listened quietly for the emergence of an answer, listening that led in part to this book. Paul says in 2 Corinthians 3:18 that as we behold the glory of the Lord, we are transformed into his image, from glory to glory. I began to hear that the development of faith is just that, a process of development, taking place over many days, years, and stages of life. I had learned a developmental perspective on the emergence of faith in James Fowler's book, *Stages of Faith*[1]; I was now learning that perspective in my experience.

I realized, through Fowler's work and my experience, that for many of us in the Western world (perhaps in our contemporary, quick culture as a whole), we want fast stuff. We don't like the reality of following in his steps (see 1 Peter 2:21) in the creation of the risen life of Christ in us. We'd rather turboboost. As I reflected on the faith, hope, and love of those whom I admired and sought to emulate, I realized that the life of a healthy Christian person is one grand adventure of growth. My mentors had come alive in Christ gradually, over time, first by their repentant departure from the dark valleys of sin, dysfunction, and failed solutions. They then walked the path of Christian development and growth, and they finally reached moments of life in the heavenly places, of life in the fullness of God's presence (Eph. 3:19).

One of the fundamental needs in this development is faith in the truth. I had wondered, what is the truth about my life now? For the question of truth, of what and whom we can trust, is not a question of fact or abstract idea or philosophy. It is a question of meaning. What does a diagnosis of cancer mean? I began to realize that a diagnosis, the reality of a transplant list, the possibility of trauma from a quite serious surgery, and the looming proximity of my mortality—these alone could not spell out the truth of my life.

For the truth of my life, the real meaning of it all, had become increasingly centered in Jesus Christ.

He was becoming the defining reality of my life. That was not my accomplishment; it was not a diploma I could hang on the wall alongside Princeton and Texas Tech. Jesus' becoming my defining reality was a gift that had come throughout the course of life, through teachers, friends, pastors, family, verses, therapists, hymns, clients, churches I had served, and churches which had served me.

I had seen others struggling with false or dysfunctional definitions of the truth of their lives. I saw them defined by others' approval, by guilt, by failure, and, yes, by cancer and others of the "thousand natural shocks that flesh is heir to" (Shakespeare).[2] But I had seen them increasingly peaceful and happy, even in the midst of troubles, their needs being fulfilled, and their questions answered, to the extent that they trusted Jesus as the defining truth of their lives. If Jesus defined them, life would be good even when it seemed or felt bad. If circumstances defined them, life could be good or bad depending on those circumstances.

They had taught me this: the truth was not just that I had cancer; the truth was that I had Jesus.

And so good would come.

I just didn't know what the good would look like. It could look like my passage to heaven; it could look like organ rejections and a provision of the grace and courage to go through chemotherapy and further surgeries; it could look like gradual deterioration in the absence of a donor organ and the grace to live out my last days with peace and gratitude for a full and rich though somewhat shortened life; it could, and did, look like a successful transplant with no rejections or complications thus far.

It would most certainly be good, because Jesus was and is and will be the truth of my life.

THE VALLEYS

When Pilate asked the almost-parenthetical question at Jesus' inquisition, it was much more than an afterthought; it was one of the most fundamental questions we walk through in the valleys of our lives: "'What is truth?'" (John 18:38).

The life that I was given through cancer can also be found in other questions of truth. Whether the path of our life is taking us through good times or bad, through wealth or poverty, through sickness or health, the underlying question is, "What defines us?" Does the truth about our life change as the circumstances of our life change? It is a powerful question because the circumstances themselves are powerful.

At times the circumstances are so powerful that they seem to overwhelm any possibility of a positive answer. How can there be any good truth in the excruciating pain of divorce, alcoholism, a father's abuse, loss of a job, or the 401K that represents a life's labor?! How can the loss of limbs or mind or face to an IED or a drunk driver—how can there be any good in the meaning, or the truth, of those tragedies?

Even Jesus asked the question: Does this death, this crucifixion mean that you, my Abba, have forsaken me?

If he asked it, it is OK if we ask it too.

The basic need is for trust, for faith that the truth is reliable and unalterable by even the most powerful of good or bad circumstances. It is not a need for an explanation, but for a transformation of the way we see life. It is not a need for miracle cures or for our lives to be arranged free of trouble and full of real good looks, money, sex, power, prestige, approval, success, and grand parties. It is a need to absorb the good news that there is no way, no day, no event, no disease, no success, nothing present, nothing to come, nothing in our past, nothing in all of created existence that can alter the truth of our lives, the truth that we don't just have our lives with all these good and bad things. We have Jesus. If our lives are held in the palm of his hand, they are—no matter how grand or troubled, pleasant or painful—very good indeed.

That is the truth that defines our lives. It defines our lives as good, even in bad experiences like cancer. But in order to acquire that trust, we usually have to let go of unsuccessful solutions, false answers to the question of truth, and powerful threats to that truth. It is necessary for us to become aware of and willing to leave the valley of despair carved by streams of *irrelevant fact, nihilism, arrogance,* and especially *rejection.*

Irrelevant Fact

The first false answer to this question is the notion that truth is fact and does not affect us. For example, Evangelical Christians have argued with great vigor, evidence, and in some cases shrill insistence that the Bible is the infallible Word of God, inspired by the Holy Spirit and containing all that is necessary to our salvation. I and those whose lives have led to this book would agree with that fact, but we know that it is possible for something to be a factual truth without becoming the truth about our lives. It is a factual truth that our car is capable of taking us to visit our family in Amarillo or friends in Dallas or mountains in Colorado. But that fact alone will never take us for a visit or a mountain vista unless we pack up, arrange the schedule, get in the car and go! And sometimes our very insistence on factual truth betrays the absence of those facts as meaningful. The Bible is the Word of God and Jesus is the Savior of the world, but those truths don't define us until we hear the Word *for ourselves* and receive the Savior as God's gift *to us*.

We fail to find the trust and truth we need when we insist on a system of answers rather than a relationship with God. Job wanted an explanation for the trouble he experienced in his valley of despair and affliction. God did not give Job an explanation. God gave Job himself.

Jesus often refused in the Gospels to give an explanation as to the truth of a problem or pain or other valley through which one of his followers was walking. He did *not* say that an Anglican or Reformed or Arminian or Neo-orthodox system is the truth of your life. He said, "*I* am the truth." God's Spirit repeated to me just before surgery for liver cancer, "I am with you; that is all you need" (2 Cor. 12:9, LB). The isolated fact or theological doctrine of God's omnipresence didn't really help to define that surgery as good in any of a number of ways. God's Spirit, whispering the truth of God's presence as I counted backwards under the infusion of anesthesia, moved me out of the valley of potential despair and toward the mountain of hope.

Nihilism

Another failed answer to the question of truth is nihilism—the ultimate denial that life, or some parts of life, could ever have a good meaning. Nihilism is a fancy way of saying that what happens in life doesn't mean anything, and it is "a tale told by an idiot, full of sound and fury signifying nothing."[3] The nihilist believes there is nothing of value. As soldiers came to say and believe concerning the horror of war in Vietnam: "It don't mean nothin'."

Sometimes we come to believe that some part of our lives, if not life as a whole, is devoid of the truth of God. I once asked a person who was having a particularly difficult time integrating sexuality and Jesus how a previous mentor would have seen Jesus' relation to sexual pleasure. He said, laughing, "My mentor didn't think Jesus had anything to do with sexual pleasure!" He was a very Christian man, but he was a sexual atheist, and didn't believe God existed as the creator and director of his sexuality.

And yet the Bible makes it clear that all of life, all thoughts, all pleasure and pain and money and sleep and anger and hope—all of life can be lived in the heavenly places of God's truth.

Arrogance

We also fail to answer the question of truth when we think we *alone* know the truth. We sometimes do this by ignorance concerning history and sometimes by isolation from other Christians whose faith may differ somewhat from ours. Either way we can arrogantly believe we are sole possessors of truth. We want, like Gollum in *The Lord of the Rings*, to say that the truth is *MINE, all mine.*

Unfortunately, some of our most enthusiastic and energetic Christian movements of the day neither know nor care about the history of those who have traveled to heavenly places before us. That can leave us dangerously vulnerable to repeating heretical, dysfunctional, and even destructively sinful distortions of the Bible. Deuteronomy 8 and many other passages in the Bible warn against forgetting the lessons of the past. Paul's letters to the Corinthians issue strong warnings against a factious, possessive attitude toward truth. It is a distortion of truth to pretend it is under sole ownership of the people called Methodist, or Catholic, or Reformed, or any other group of the people of God. The truth of our lives does not lie in a group or set of doctrines.

Jesus, and Jesus only, is the truth of our lives.

Rejection

The most powerful assault on the truth of our lives occurs in traumatic rejection. We will deal with this issue further in chapter 14, but it is important to mention here because it is so prevalent in life and in the Bible. Again and again, God speaks through the biblical writers to normalize the painful experience of doubting, even denying, the truth of our lives when the loud, shrill voices of people and events around us seem to throw that truth under the heel of Satan. Jesus called John the Baptist the greatest prophet born among women. But even he asked when he faced rejection and eventual execution at the hands of Herod, "Are you the one who is to come, or should we expect someone else?" (Matt. 11:3).

The valley of rejection can come from parents, our own failure, car wrecks, disease, financial ruin, divorce, friends, colleagues, addiction, or any of the other blows that life can bring. But when rejection comes, as it came to John the Baptist, we can easily wonder: Is Jesus really, *really* the truth of our lives? If he *is* the truth of our lives, where is the path out of the valley of doubt toward the heavenly places of assurance?

THE PATHS

What are some of the markers, the cairns, that show the path to the heavenly places of truth? God can use many experiences and instruments to give us the truth of our lives, but there are five that stand out and encompass all the others: *communion, worship, truth-testing, wisdom,* and *the Holy Spirit*.

Communion

The first gift Jesus left to sustain our relationship with Him as the defining truth of our lives was not the Bible, nor a book, nor a denomination. It certainly was not a theological system. Jesus gave the gifts of the Holy Spirit and the sacraments of baptism—and communion. In my own experience, God has used four gifts to keep my life together even in days when it most seemed to be falling apart: the outdoors, the devotional *Daily Light on the Daily Path,*[4] a few key relationships—and holy communion. Although I am not Roman Catholic and am actually rather Anglican in my beliefs about communion, I do believe that something spiritually powerful occurs when that bread and wine enter the body of a believer. Those elements say to us, as often as we eat that bread and drink that cup, that Christ is in us and we are in Him. Communion is a cairn, it is the one of the first and most essential cairns, leading us forward out of the valley of the shadow of death into the heavenly places in Christ Jesus.

Sacramental experiences other than communion can also contribute to defining our life in Christ. These are elements of common life, such as baptismal water, communion bread, or the pages of a Bible, that God uses to say, "You are mine and this is my gift to you." Music, food, work, play, rest, grandchildren, flowers, a spring day, snowflakes, cool water––all the good things of life can feed the truth that God is with us and we belong to him, that he is our home.

My dad was a child of the Depression and to this day I can hear the genuine tone of his gratitude for food, no matter how simple. Food was a cairn leading him up the trail to the heavenly places in Christ. He heard the truth that he was loved by God through the nourishment which was often deficient during the Depression but became available later.

Worship

Worship as a whole, not only in the administration and reception of the sacraments and the sacramental, is also a marker that can lead us forward. And it must be said that the worship which engenders trust in the truth in Jesus is not adoration of a preacher or a band or an architectural marvel.

Worship is the adoration of God. If a preacher or a band or a building witness to Jesus as the truth of our lives, then listen to the preacher, go to the building, enjoy the band. But the truth we need, the trust we so desperately seek, cannot be contained by a denomination or a preacher or a band; it is contained in the *only* way, truth, and life; it is contained only in relationship with Jesus.

One of the best biblical examples of worship is Mary, the sister of Martha (see Luke 10:38–42). Martha would have fit well into the Western world; she was busy taking care of stuff that needed to be done. Mary, on the other hand, "sat at the Lord's feet listening to what he said" (Luke 10:39). Hers is the worship that marks the way to the heavenly places.

There was a period in my own life which was particularly dark, in which I often didn't know which way was up. I was dealing with the final stages of functional alcoholism and was quite lost in a quagmire of self-loathing and confusion, trying one unsuccessful solution after another. At the time I had a rather good job in social services, and since I was a *functional* alcoholic, I seldom missed work. During lunch I would often go sit in an Episcopal church sanctuary where the organist usually practiced during my lunchtime. I didn't know what to pray, didn't know what to think, didn't know where I was going; but to this day I deeply believe that those hours of worship, simply sitting in the presence of God, became one of the cairns marking the path to the sobriety I enjoy today.

Wisdom

Another source of guidance toward fulfilled life in the heavenly places is the witness of wisdom. There is a picture in my office of my paternal grandfather, a mule named Bill, and me when I was eight years old. I don't keep that picture because of my grandfather's education—he was only able to attend formal schooling through the sixth grade. And he wasn't a perfect man—he had a ferocious temper and never could manage what little money there was. I only spent about thirty or forty days altogether with him in my youth, but he was for me, in his personal presence, spirit of gratitude for life, love of beauty, and zeal for the gospel, a witness of wisdom.

His was not the wisdom of principle or precept; it was the wisdom of a relationship of love that affected me and my vision of life in a powerful way. Granddad and my relationship with him became a cairn, a marker pointing me toward the heavenly places in Christ. And I have found that many students, clients, and church folk have a person like Granddad who can function as a cairn, a marker of the path toward the heavenly places of truth.

Truth-Testing

It is important also to examine the claims to truth, to test the spirits (see 1 John 4:1). It is not good to be blown around with every idea that sounds appealing. We cannot take in the word of a grandfather, denomination, theologian, the way we were raised, or anyone else as an infallible spokesperson for God. The Methodist quadrilateral is a way of examining claims to truth and is not a bad way to test thoughts, ideas, influences for their reliability and validity.[5] The four resources for testing claims to truth, or quadrilateral, consist of: (1) the dominant message of Scripture, (2) the message of the historic church, (3) logic or reasonableness, and (4) the Holy Spirit in personal experience. I would also add another test of the claim to truth: (5) what is the *effect* of a belief, idea, or other claim to truth?

There are two examples of common Christian beliefs that cannot stand up to the quadrilateral tests: (1) the belief that I must be or can be perfect, and (2) the belief that my life is doomed by some past event. Perfectionism and guilt are two very common, debilitating, unbiblical, and irrational dispositions that lead to inertia, irresponsibility, and depression. The message of the Bible is that we are forgiven and accepted in Christ in such a way that we can live in newness of life in the risen Christ, not perfectly, but in growth toward the maturity which is life in the heavenly places. When we can absorb the witness of wisdom from family, friends, ministers, and counselors, then distill that witness by the tests above, that witness can be a well-built cairn pointing our journey upward toward fullness of life in Christ.

The Holy Spirit

The work of the Holy Spirit is simply to bring Jesus Christ to life in the experience of those who follow Christ. There are two passages which I have found consistently useful in clarifying the work of the Spirit: John 14:26 and John 16:12–14. Those passages give us the assurance that God's Spirit is at work in us to infuse his Word into our lives and to help us understand what is going on in our lives to help us grow up into Christ in all things. John 14 speaks specifically of the Spirit activating our memory of Jesus' teaching. This is a reference not just to the words of Jesus in the New Testament, but to the message of God's life-giving love in the birth, death, resurrection, and presence of Jesus Christ in all our lives. And John 16 promises that the Spirit will show us what is going on in our lives. John 16:13 has often been translated in terms of the future which will unfold in Christ. But the Greek expression (*ta erchomena)* can and I believe does refer to the Spirit showing us what is going on when we go through some of life's good, bad, or just plain ordinary experiences. In simple terms, the Holy Spirit illuminates what God is up to in our lives in light of the teaching, work, and presence of Jesus Christ.

A large part of *Climbing Home* is devoted to pointing out the ways in which God can use simple things like sleep, exercise, food, work, and play in our journey toward the heavenly places. When that happens, and when God shows that even cancer cannot define us but that Jesus can define our cancer, God's Spirit is showing us what is really going on in our lives. There are many cairns which can mark the path of truth out of our valleys and into fullness of life. But each of these cairns provides different forms of the same thing: a trustworthy definition of our life in our relationship to Jesus Christ. And even when our need for the truth of our lives occurs in the deepest valleys of doubt and denial, these cairns of communion, worship, wise counsel, and careful testing of claims to truth have clarified the path for many whose experience underlies this book. Through them all, God's Spirit can, if we listen, speak the word of the truth of our lives: "You not only have the good and the bad of your life; you not only have your relationships, your gains and losses, your cancer and your transplant, your strength and your weakness. Above all you have Jesus Christ; and in him you have a good, a very good life."

Influences of all sorts seek to define us; some are called "principalities (and) powers" (Eph. 6:12, NKJV) or "trouble or hardship or persecution or famine or nakedness or danger or sword" (Rom. 8:35). But the truth of God, leading us upward past the cairns of sacrament, worship, the witness of wisdom, and the message of Scripture, is that our life is "hidden with Christ in God" (Col. 3:3), that "Christ lives in (us)…" (Gal. 2:20). Because that is the truth of our lives, because our relationship with Jesus is completely trustworthy, we can experience all of the other questions and needs of this book, and all of the questions and Scriptures and needs not in this book but present in our lives, as a cup held under the waterfall of the Christ "[Whose] love has been poured out into our hearts through the Holy Spirit" (Rom. 5:5).

THE HEAVENLY PLACES

So what does it look like to live the truth of life as defined by Jesus? When life in the heavenly places permeates our lives, we, quite simply, grow toward the image of Jesus Christ in all things (see Eph. 4:15). *He* is what we look like when we live in the heavenly places, in the mountains of hope in his truth.

There is an old word that's not heard much anymore, but it's a good part of Christian life and characterizes life defined by the truth of God––the word *godliness*. Perhaps the word is avoided because we run like scalded dogs from bigheaded arrogance, and rightly so. Perhaps the concept of godliness is avoided because we're scared it would keep us from having fun or making money or enjoying good sex. But godliness is not a matter of long faces or moral superiority; it is being like the one who shows what we're made to be; it's being like Christ; it's being who we really are. The word translated "godliness" is used primarily in First and Second Timothy in contrast to a *false* godliness which denies the functions of earth and body as good. True godliness involves experiencing every dimension of our lives—body, money, athletics, mind, relationships, work, aging, and play—all as the arena of developing Christlikeness.

Life in the truth means we "walk just as He walked" (1 John 2:6, NKJV). It means we think like, work like, love like, enjoy life like, play like, and generally live like Christ. This doesn't mean a guilt-driven perfectionism and it sure doesn't mean every dimension of our lives must be religious. It means that God's intention for humankind in creation is worked out in us as God's new creation.

Life in the truth is what this book is all about. *Climbing Home* is a handbook of healthy Christian living as a process. We emerge in that process from the valleys of questions, needs, and failed answers; we then walk past the cairns that mark the path upward; and we finally experience increasing degrees of life in the heavenly places of hope fulfilled, where we are who we're meant to be.

THE QUESTIONS AND SCRIPTURES

1. What do you see as the defining truth of your life (for example, a traumatic event, your parents, Gospel of John, a minister)?
2. How do you need or want to change the way you see your life (for example, more honesty, less self-criticism, more positive thinking and speaking)?
3. What does God see as the defining truth of your life (for example, as sinful, as alive in Christ, as struggling)?
4. What verses, actions, or people could help you define your life as God sees it (for example, Isaiah 40–62, Philippians, 1 John, a counselor, exercise)?
5. What will you do today to move toward God's truth for your life?
6. Scripture for further reflection: Deut. 8:2–18; Prov. 3:5–6; John 8:12–32, 14:1–16:33; Cor. 1:18–3:23; 1 John 4:1–6.

CHAPTER 2

HOME: WHERE DO I BELONG?

They called it Sacred Harp Singing.[1] We got out of Granddad's old Ford and walked toward the Brilliant Freewill Baptist Church surrounded by a sound like none my eight-year-old ears had ever heard. I can still feel the July heat and North Alabama humidity seeping into my pores; I can smell the sweet and salty scent of red clay as we approached the church; I can feel the weight of the basket of chicken and corn and fried okra and biscuits I carried; but above all I can hear the sounds of another world, perhaps a heavenly place. It felt, at least for a while, like I was surrounded by home.

Yet I didn't know where my home really was. I knew where I lived with my family, but there seemed to be so many places competing for the title of home.

My mother set the table of our Alabama home with a tablecloth which was decorated with a map of Texas; there was a helium balloon in the panhandle, a bucking horse around Pecos, and a depiction of the Alamo in San Antonio. That tablecloth prompted stories of my birthplace, just three blocks from that shrine to those who gave their lives fighting for Texas' independence in the early spring of 1836. My Mom's wistful memories of San Antone during World War II left me feeling that surely Texas, not Alabama, was home. And so, many years later, when I moved my family to west Texas to do doctoral work in marriage and family therapy, I felt that was home.

But, soon after our move to Texas, when my family and I first sat in awe on Brown's Pass in Colorado, looking across the valley toward the Three Apostles on the Continental Divide, I felt that was surely home. I came to believe that I was most at home in the outdoors, that trees and sky were my true roof, that streams and trails marked my true path, that the untrammeled world of God's creation was home. Love for the outdoors as home began in early childhood, expanded in the Boy Scouts, continued in the hills where I grew up, and reached an apex on Brown's Pass in 1990. "Surely," I thought, "my home is in the outdoors."

But then there were the Sunday nights at First Methodist Church in Birmingham, Alabama, especially the nights when we were served communion. I remember sitting particularly close to some of the girls when I was twelve or thirteen and their proximity and the solemnity of the service left me feeling that surely I was then close to heaven, close to home.

So I seemed to have many, sometimes quite disparate, places that I called home.

I developed the question of all who live in a mobile society, a question as old as Abraham and as recent as the moving sign down the street: Where do I belong? Where is my home?

THE VALLEYS

The questions that clients, church members, students, friends, and family have raised about their lives are almost always simple but challenging, none more than the question of where we belong. The need for belonging is not just a desire for a roof, an origin, or a genealogy. It is a need for the connections in which all our other questions and needs are met. The place of belonging, our home, is where we ask the questions that can unveil the needs for safety, for hope, for love, for purpose.

The illustration of my shifting sense of home raises the question we ask and the need we feel: where are we most from? What is the place where we can quench our thirst for belonging? Robert Frost raised this question beautifully in his poem *West-Running Brook.* A husband and wife are conversing about a brook and the way it runs, eddies, and flows. Toward the end of the conversation the husband says, after being prompted by his wife to speak further:

> Our life runs down in sending up the clock.
> The brook runs down in sending up our life.
> The sun runs down in sending up the brook.

And there is something sending up the sun.
It is this backward motion toward the source,
Against the stream, that most we see ourselves in,
The tribute of the current to the source.
It is from this in nature we are from.
It is most us.[2]

We yearn for home, the place that is most us, the place we are most from.

But if our home is a place in the valley of the shadow of death, the powerful need for a good home intensifies the pain of an unhappy home. Our self-made answers to this need to belong can bring about some of our most dramatic failures. Some of those failures emerge from our families of origin, some from attempts to replace or supplement our families of origin.

The culture of the southeastern part of the United States, where I grew up, often praises "the way I was raised." But ministers and counselors have seen the way a person is raised can destroy life rather than enhance life. And it is not just the experiences of abuse, abandonment, or otherwise distorted relationships that can leave a child feeling that home is a place of pain rather than a place to learn good life. Families of origin can breed perfectionism, paranoia, lust, greed, self-pity, and can foment a sense of belonging to darkness and death rather than light and life. Home in those cases can be erected in the valley of despair and can feel like a trap, keeping us away from good life.

Thomas Hardy's novel, *The Mayor of Casterbridge*, portrays the life of Elizabeth Jane Farfrae who experienced an extraordinarily painful existence until her marriage to Donald Farfrae, with whom she found a home with peace and joy.[3] But the defining power of her childhood pain lingered. At the end of the novel, Hardy says,…"in being forced to class herself among the fortunate she did not cease to wonder at the persistence of the unforeseen, when the one to whom such unbroken tranquility had been accorded in the adult stage was she whose youth had seemed to teach that happiness was but the occasional episode in a general drama of pain."[4]

There are many examples of dysfunctional attempts to correct and replace a painful family of origin: Gang membership, ethnic superiority, nostalgic return to a better era, serial marriages, self-righteous adherence to a cult, and materialism all represent efforts to build a home that is better than what childhood provided. Those who work in the helping professions are often amazed at the power of a cult or gang or obsessive adherence to a corporate tower of Babel. That power is a clear indicator of the depth of our need for belonging, for home.

Many years ago I was privileged to work in an agency which provided service to runaway youth. Nearly all of these young people had been abused, and it was a credit to the board which supported that agency that our work with law enforcement and others did not require returning these kids back home. Of course there were times that returning home was a good course of action. But these runaways, and many of us who have sought to escape the trauma of dysfunctional homes without running away, all needed to find the path to a true home, a place of belonging with love and nurture and life enhancement.

Of course, most of us grow up in homes that are neither hell on earth nor a microcosm of heaven. We grow up with a mixture of good and hurtful elements in our family of origin, both the life-giving and life-draining. And so we are left wondering, at times by our families of origin, at times by dysfunctional replacements or supplements to our childhood, where is our true home? Where are we *most* from?

THE PATHS

An old drunk, spending the night in jail, sings symbolically in the movie version of *A River Runs Through It*, "Show me the way to go home, I'm tired and I want to go to bed…."[5] And don't we all want to know the way to go home?

There are several realms that God gives as cairns to mark the path toward home; these include *church*, *family*, *place*, and *ritual*. Unfortunately, a disclaimer is in order. For, as we saw above concerning family of origin, each of these can represent a painful destruction of belonging, of true home. Church, for example, can render unbiblical, blasphemous judgment as well as the gift of belonging. And the Old Testament designates some places as a poor choice to live, such as Sodom and Gomorrah. We need to ask, in seeking the way to go home, what the cairns of church, family, place, and ritual look like when they are healthy, life-giving trail markers.

Family

God designs family to be a microcosm of the kingdom of God. Family can grow toward an earthly realm in which all of the qualities of the heavenly places in this book are represented. There are four qualities in particular which can make family a place of true home: nurture, play, strength, and direction.

It is important to say here that family serves best when it is an instrument of God rather than an idol as god. Healthy family esteem is a good thing. But narcissistic arrogance, a sense of superiority to others, can destroy the "family" cairn that could otherwise point to our home in the heavenly places in Christ. Family is at its best when there is not only love *within* the family but also *from* the family to others.

Church

Church is a place where family belonging can be extended to include others. Church is a network of relationships beyond biological family where we can experience the nurture, play, strength, and direction of the family of God. Sometimes church can occur at a place of worship. I have also found that many people experience church in places other than a church building: a community Bible study, a friendship, a relationship with a spiritual mentor who may not even be a member of one's denomination, a camp counselor, perhaps a teacher or coach. One of our sons is both a pastor and a teacher. Soon after he was appointed to two United Methodist churches, I asked him where his churches were. He astutely answered, "Dad, church is really wherever the people of God are; so it's at school, it's with my kids, and it's at 'church.'" Then he told me the physical location of the places he would be serving. But he had correctly indicated that church is wherever two or three or more folks are gathered in Christ's name.

Social media can also contribute to a Christian experience of church.

The history of the church is sprinkled with instances of God's using secular events, languages, clothing, technology, and many other aspects of the development of human life. Sometimes Christian groups have seen some of these developments as inherently worldly or otherwise inconsistent with life in the kingdom of God. The Amish see the internal combustion engine or the television as ungodly, and I sometimes think they have a point! But generally the human tools of living such as cars, coffee makers, the Greek language, indoor plumbing, and social media can be used in godly ways. For example, part of my wife's "church" includes folks all over the country, from Montana to Alabama, from Presbyterian to nondenominational, from contemporary worshipers to folks who spurn organized religion. I have seen the enrichment of her church life through this breadth of church connection by way of social media.

Place

The diversity of places we live through electronic communication does not replace the need for geographical place as a part of home. Each of us can find a place to live that gives us a unique sense of home. For God's people in the Old Testament, that place was Canaan, the land of promise given to Abraham and his descendants. For folk in pioneer America, that place was often represented by a homestead. For some it is a house, for others a geographical area like upstate New York or the delta woods of Mississippi or the Serengeti of Africa. It is often difficult for the members of a mobile society to identify a place or places that represent home, that mark the path home.

Sometimes in our modern world the place cairn of our walk home needs to travel with us. That certainly was the case with the Ark of the Covenant which went with the Israelites during their nomadic times in the desert. The holy place, the place of home in the presence of God, accompanied God's people in their travels. For us it may be a Bible, a prayer chair, a piece of furniture, even a family altar. Although it was difficult for my mother to move from a house to varying degrees of medically assisted living, three things never left her: her devotional book, a piano keyboard, and her prayer chair. She took those places of home with her until she departed for her final home.

Ritual

Home can grow stronger when it includes ritual. There are some groups which attend to the rituals of home more than others, and perhaps this is one of the missing cairns of contemporary life. The Jewish Shabbat meal on Friday night is a good example of this kind of ritual. One of our sons engages in this kind of ritual most nights when their family sings a hymn, reads Scripture, and kneels to pray. This ritual is helping this family develop and maintain a sense of belonging, of home.

A similar ritual was part of my visits to my paternal grandparents' home; I can still feel the heat, smell the smells, and hear my grandmother's whispered prayers as Granddad read from a huge King James Bible, then knelt to pray for his family and life, for the world, and for his home to remain a heavenly place. And the next day, when we went to the Sacred Harp singin' and dinner on the grounds, I also felt at home.

THE HEAVENLY PLACES

In a way, the heavenly places of home and belonging are in heaven itself. But we can also experience something of home before we "go home." There are three qualities of the heavenly places of home here on earth: *blessing*, *community*, and *leadership*.

Blessing

Jesus gives blessing. This "blessedness" of Jesus' teaching (Matt. 5–7, Luke 6) and throughout the Bible refers to the happiness we all seek. The Greek and Hebrew terms translated *blessing* or *blessed* are used in secular literature primarily regarding the well-being and happiness of the gods of the ancient world. Biblical sources use this term to refer to the sense that life is good among the people of God, in the home of God. And so Paul says in the opening of his letter to the Ephesian Christians: "Blessed be the God and Father of our Lord Jesus Christ, who has blessed us with every spiritual blessing in the heavenly places in Christ" (Eph. 1:3, NKJV).

One sometimes hears in Christian teaching that God does not give happiness, but rather joy. This may be a difference of semantics, but it's really more than that. The blessing that can attend the dwelling place of

God is a matter of choice. Joy is happiness which can continue independent of unhappy circumstances. The book *Happiness Is a Lifestyle* by Frank Minirth, MD is a significant contribution to the understanding that happiness does not just *come upon* us; it is something we can *choose*.[6] The possibility of choosing happiness is also part of what has been called the Positive Psychology movement. But the attempts to achieve happiness by purely secular means such as diet, yoga, exercise, self-esteem, music, or massage are often like cut flowers—quite attractive, but lacking the staying power of a well-rooted experience of blessing in Christ's heavenly places.

Secular means of happiness can be used by God as a part of blessing. There is a difference, though, a crucial difference, between the blessing of God and a blessing which stands on its own. As Proverbs says, "The blessing of the Lord brings wealth, without painful toil for it" (Prov. 10:22). And so yoga and diet and exercise and positive psychology, when they are rooted in Christ, can be like social media rooted in Christ, appliances of the home of God.

Community

The blessing of God is always tied to intimacy with God and with the community of God's people. The association between these three elements of the heavenly places of belonging is clearest in the letters of 1 John and Philippians. There are two important New Testament words in this association: *koinonia* and *chara,* or, loosely translated, "fellowship" and "joy." The use of these words and their associated contexts in Philippians and 1 John shows that it is possible even in quite difficult circumstances to live with the inner comforts and pleasures of the heavenly places. Philippians was written from prison, and both letters were composed in a time of dissension in the church and persecution in the world. Yet each makes it abundantly clear that Christian people can celebrate a sense of belonging and of happy life in the home of God by loving God, each other, and life in the *blessing*, *intimacy*, and *community* of the heavenly places. Many of those who serve in the church see this creation of home in hospitals, funeral homes, pastoral visitation, meals, and other ways that church gathers to share the life of Christ's fellowship.

Leadership

Finally, God's home is a place of structure through leadership and obedience. These are probably two of the most misunderstood and at times misused words in Christian life, for they are often used in terms of the controllers (leaders) and the controlled (the obedient). Family dynamics, as observed by marriage and family therapists, reveals many de facto leaders and followers in any family, church, or other group setting. Every parent knows that at 3:00 AM in the morning, even a sick baby can be in charge of how much sleep a father or mother gets that night! Structural family therapy has been developed around the notion that at times the power, authority, and obedience distribution in a home can be either destructive and dysfunctional or helpful and life-giving. God intends for family structure to be life-enhancing for all in that family.

Each of us is called as part of God's home to be a leader and to be obedient. Leadership does not belong only to fathers and pastors and obedience does not belong only to children. There is a very significant verse in Ephesians which opens the familiar passage concerning husbands loving their wives as Christ loves the church and wives being subject to their husbands as the church is to Christ: "Submit *to one another* out of reverence for Christ" (Eph. 5:21, italics added).

Two structural principles of God's home can maintain healthy belonging: (1) Leadership is always carried out in obedience to God and loving service to those who are led; (2) Obedience is never an end in itself but is designed to contribute to Christlikeness. Leadership without obedience is hollow control. Obedience without becoming like Christ, without growing up into servant leaders, is incomplete, just rote repetition. These two principles are joined in a simple question: what would it look like for me to receive and reflect Jesus Christ in the community of people I'm with at this time?

A powerful example of this blend of leadership and obedience is Jesus' washing the disciples' feet in John 13; in that simple act he is both the leader giving an example to his disciples and an obedient servant, submitting to his Father and to the needs of his disciples. And he shows that in the heavenly places, our true home and place of belonging, he is the center of the circle of his people, who follow him in doing for each other what he has done for us.

THE QUESTIONS AND SCRIPTURES

1. What three places have you felt the most comfortable in your life (for example, taking a nap after church, fishing as a child, etc.)?
2. What three places have given you the most nurture (for example, at communion, in devotions, with your father, etc.)?
3. What three places has God had the most influence in your life (for example, in your youth group, with your closest friend, in the woods, etc.)?
4. Where does God make others feel the most comfortable and nurtured through you (for example, with your children, in Sunday School, at work, etc.)?
5. After reading this chapter, what do you believe God would like to improve in your life this year? What would he like for home to mean in your life (for example, letting my spouse feel more comfort/nurture when with me, reaching out to a sibling across the country, etc.)?
6. Scripture for further reflection: Ps. 127, 137; Prov. 31:10–31; Matt. 5–7; Eph. 4:1–16, 5:21–6:4.

CHAPTER 3

IDENTITY: WHO AM I?

When Jesus began to teach, heal, and call people to new life with a power that was uncommon in his day, people asked, "Who is this man?" (Mark. 4:41, TLB). It is one of the initial questions we ask when someone has a powerful impact in sports, work, love, or church. It is one of the most fundamental questions we ask about our own lives.

When I was a boy I "became" several different people in the process of discovering my identity. My family had to call me "engineer" when I was five years old, or I wouldn't come to the table. I had a fascination with trains—their size, their noisy power, their steam, their huge wheels, their firebox, and whistle and bells, and chug, chug, chug way of starting slowly then gathering that spellbinding momentum as they charged down the tracks. I had a great uncle who had been killed in a train wreck and a step-grandfather who worked for the Southern Railroad, and I lived in a town connected to the rest of the country by trains. And so I "became" an engineer. It was my identity.

But then I began to find new identities. I discovered the west and "became" Roy Rogers. That was one of my first "new births." Then I became my paternal grandfather's protégé. Then came Boy Scouts, and I became an outdoorsman. Then I became a runner, perhaps even a future Olympic miler, like Roger Bannister.

Next I began attempting to integrate some of the people I had become. I discovered horses. My first "real" job was cleaning out horse stalls, hauling hay, and doing other odd jobs on a farm. That job allowed me to combine the outdoors, my grandfather's influence, athleticism, and my budding young hormonal yearning for masculinity. I would lean against a fence at the end of the day during that first summer's work, and I would picture myself becoming a farmer or rancher, perhaps out west somewhere. Years later, during my first year of doctoral work at Texas Tech University, when it came my turn to share why I had chosen to attend a school in dusty, remote west Texas, I said, chuckling at my honesty, I thought I was still trying to become a cowboy! It still felt like part of my identity.

But all the roles I had taken on—engineer, outdoorsman, rancher, athlete, etc.—only confused the issue of my basic identity. For the heart of a role is imitation; the heart of identity is being. Identity is not a matter of what one *does* or *looks like,* but of what one *is*.

There was a psychotherapist in Mobile, Alabama who helped me with the need for identity. It was a six o'clock session, and my counselor asked me to let my wife know it would be an extended time. The therapist knew it was time for me to know my identity as distinct from the many roles I had played. By that time I was an ordained United Methodist minister, a husband and father, and a recovering alcoholic. I was an avid reader of theology and biblical commentaries. I still pursued outdoor activities, loved classical music, and was developing some dimensions of my identity in my family. But I identified parts of who I was rather than the core of my identity.

My counselor had me sit in various places around her office. There was a place for the minister, the son in my family of origin, the husband and father, the outdoorsman, the alcoholic, and the student. Each of these engaged in conversation with each of the others; and it was rather fun and lively. After a while it became apparent that someone was missing, and the therapist eventually asked, "You are having a good conversation among all the parts of your life, but what of you? There is a minister, a student, a husband and father, a son…but where is Madoc?" For the remainder of those three hours I began to know a core identity, a definition, of a person called Madoc who could both embrace all of those roles but who was more than any of them.

I needed to see what God had envisioned when he chose to create me, when he first breathed into me the breath of life. I needed, and we all need, to know more than function or job or even relationships. The need for identity is the need to answer the question of ourselves that people asked about Jesus: "Who is this person?"

THE VALLEYS

The failed answers to that question fall into one or more of four categories: *possession*, *function*, *ability*, and *achievement*. If those are positive, we feel we are somebody, and we have a positive identity. If, especially, these four areas bring us accolades from other folks, we can puff out our chest and say, "My, what a good girl/boy am I!" If we feel we have no real function, are poor, lack talent, and haven't achieved much, we can feel we aren't worth much. But these failed solutions are based on insecure foundations. They carve out yet another canyon of despair.

Possessions and Function

The trap of *possessions* and defining ourselves by our *function* is a valley that obstructs many dimensions of our journey to the heavenly places in Christ Jesus. Jesus said, "…life does not consist in an abundance of possessions" (Luke 12:15). Yet men sometimes limit their sense of worth to what they have and what they earn in order to have more.

The valley of *possessions* and *function* can plague women as well, as for example, when they see their identity largely in terms of the looks they *possess* and the motherhood in which they *function*. And when children leave home, especially if their departure coincides with a decline of a mother's attractiveness, women can feel they have lost their identity. They can feel they have no more worth.

Several years ago during my training as a marriage and family therapist I was privileged to work with a family that had a pretty severe financial problem. It turned out that the parents earned plenty and the two children were not particularly extravagant in their demands. But this family's spending seemed to consistently exceed their income. There seemed to be a systemic belief in the family, especially in the parents, that if they had just a little more extravagant TV screen size, higher-priced cars, and better-quality clothes, their worth would be assured. They were a quite devoted Christian family and they were growing into an awareness of their worth in Jesus Christ. It took some work for them to crawl out of the valley of worth through *possessions*, but they did it. They actually developed an almost countercultural sense that their identity in Christ was so far beyond the stuff they once craved that they became rather frugal.

Ability

Men can easily feel their identity is dependent on work and the *ability* to take their families on vacations and to buy cars and boats and stuff. If earnings decline or job loss occurs or inflation erodes spending power, those men can feel they have lost their lives. And sometimes, even at the cost of their families' well-being, men seek a solution to the insignificance of what they have by building something more. They tear down their first barns and build bigger barns (see Luke 12:18). And when the insecure foundation of barn-building in its various forms leaves them destitute, they feel a gnawing worthlessness.

The decline of *abilities* with the aging process is particularly threatening to identity in our society. If either men or women attach identity to the ability to sing or play football or do woodworking or create art, the loss of those abilities can feel like the loss of identity. This loss of identity through loss of ability is particularly insidious in loss of sexual ability because we have created a culture in which youthful sexual ability is equated with hefty identity and worth. We have drifted far from previous cultures in which the elderly were venerated and appreciated for their life-experience-enriched identities.

Achievement

Jesus' parable of the sheep and the goats in Matthew 25 is a powerful correction of our sense of significant *achievement.* You may remember that Jesus told this parable in the context of his growing conflict with the religious leaders who would eventually call for his crucifixion. The parable is a key indicator, along with John 14–17, of the things Jesus considered most significant to leave with the disciples before his death. What are the greatest achievements in God's eyes? Acts of love, kindness, and provision for people like prisoners, the naked, thirsty, alone—"one of the least of these brothers and sisters of mine" (see Matthew 25:40).

If most of us think back over our lives we realize that some of the most influential, positive events in our development have come from actions that would not be considered particularly grand and glorious. We may think that the most important contributions we make in life are socially, financially, or vocationally noteworthy. But Jesus teaches that those things fail to answer our need to really be somebody, to have a significant identity. He stands our sense of identity through bigger and better achievements on its head. He shows us that *achievement* is a failed source of stable identity.

There was a recent NFL football game in which a well-known quarterback was, as usual, cheered and applauded for his prowess and triumphs on the field. He had become aware that a disabled child had acquired an opportunity to attend the game on the sidelines and see his hero play. Before the game, the quarterback went over to the sidelines and spent several minutes with the child. Afterward he indicated that those few minutes were more important than anything he would do on the field. That represents the sense of significant achievement Jesus spoke of in Matthew 25. It is not usually the case, but occasionally athletes, actors, ministers, and others with public notoriety show a realization that identity through the grandiosities of life is a valley of despair. When someone like that quarterback, a Christian major league baseball pitcher, or an opera singer, genuinely reaches out to the least of those among us, they are witnesses to the path out of the valley of despair and toward the heavenly places of the mountain of hope.

THE PATHS

There are four cairns on the path to the heavenly places of identity in Christ: *new birth*, *dominant relationships*, *detachment, driving strength*, and *deepest desires.*

New Birth

New birth defines us as belonging to and coming from God as well as our family of origin. I have had the privilege of working as a counselor with a number of people whose family of origin has ranged from chaotic to insidiously destructive. Their adoption into the family of God through new birth has been particularly meaningful. But for any of us to try to pinpoint the exact moment of new birth may be not only unnecessary but inconsistent with Jesus' use of that term (see John 3). We do not know the exact moment of our spiritual conception any more than we know the exact moment of our physical conception. But we can be grateful that the root of our identity has all the stability of God himself. We are born of him.

There is a dimension of the *new birth* that is sometimes omitted from our evangelistic focus on that experience. Brennan Manning has written a wonderful work which can open this dimension for the Christian community: *Abba's Child.*[1] This book helps us to understand that our birth into the family of God gives us access to an ongoing intimacy with the father of that birth. I have seen several people, men especially, whose lives have been transformed by a realization that their identity in Christ does not depend on their earthly family of origin. Our identity can emerge from an intimate relationship with a playful, powerful, wise, gentle, life-giving and life-enhancing Abba, our heavenly daddy through *new birth.*

Dominant Relationships

There is a saying in Alcoholics Anonymous that recovery, changing identity from alcoholic to sober, includes changing "playmates and playgrounds." The *dominant relationships* of our identity in Christ also change. We saw in the last chapter that church is a network of relationships in which we experience the nurture, play, strength, and direction of the family of God. Some of those relationships become dominant in helping us understand who we are in Christ. I can think of at least twelve folks who have been particularly influential in teaching me my identity in Christ; they include my paternal grandfather, my wife, my five children, a therapist, a counselor where I was in treatment for alcoholism, and some teachers. And I have learned many layers of my identity in Christ from those I have served; the help I have given has returned to enhance my own life. These have been my mentors, cairns on the path to my identity in Christ.

Spiritual direction is a practice in contemporary Christian discipleship which can be a helpful part of growing into our identity in Christ. A spiritual director can become one of those *dominant relationships* in our identity formation. But spiritual direction is not spiritual control. There are times when the practice of spiritual direction (or sponsorship in Twelve Step programs) can become an ego trip for the mentor and subservient dependency in the mentee. Spiritual direction at its best is walking the path to the heavenly places together under the direction of God's Spirit. The difference is that the mentor has walked the path before and can point out some of the crevasses, the box canyons, the places of refreshment, and can provide encouragement on the way. My wife and I have developed a habit we dearly love as we walk to a restaurant or movie or church; she loves to take my arm as we walk, not for me to control her or because she can't walk on her own, but as an act of companionship. That's a picture of spiritual direction.

Detachment

There are other relationships which call for *detachment* in order for us to become who we really are in Christ. There was a time when I thought the passages about loving not (for example, 1 John 2:15) or separating from the world (for example, 2 Corinthians 6:17) were for old fogeys and folks who weren't any fun. Maybe it's because I myself am an old fogey now, but my assessment of those passages has changed, largely from lessons learned from clients, students, and church members. There are some relationships which can just drain the life out of you. God does not say not to love and serve these folks; but Jesus *did* say that if we go to a place or relationship which does not receive who we are and what we have to give, it can be the better part of wisdom to dust off our feet and go on down the road (see Matthew 10:14). *Detachment* from what drains us and *attachment* to what gives us life are stones in an important cairn on the path to identity in Christ.

Driving Strengths

And the *driving strengths* of our lives can provide another cairn on the path to our identity in Christ. There are several techniques which have been devised to help people discover their spiritual gifts. But a word or two of caution are in order. First, the strengths of our lives are fluid; they are not the same at ten, thirty, and seventy years of age. And second, we need to be sure that what we or others see as strengths are the same as what God considers as strengths. Some may see it as a quality of strength to win, to have control, to overpower an opponent in business or athletics or politics, or to argue down a spouse. But what the world considers strength may be weakness when it comes to growing up into Christ's identity in us. The question we need to ask is, "What are the ways in which I am most gifted, most capable of lifting others up to be what they can be in Christ?" That is the strength of identity in Christ.

For example, my wife and I both seek to be servants in ministry. But our *driving strengths* are very different. She crochets, bakes bread, has borne children, and as a nurse started IV's and changed bandages. I have preached, taught, written, and counseled. But I have never borne a child and she has never written a doctoral dissertation. We are both seeking to grow up into Christ in all things (see Ephesians 4:15), but because God has given us different strengths we are not exactly alike in our growth or identity.

Deepest Desires

Our *deepest desires* can also be an indicator of who we are in Christ. Psalm 37 links our desires and God's formation of his will in us:

> Trust in the Lord and do good;
> dwell in the land and enjoy safe pasture.
> Take delight in the Lord,
> and he will give you the desires of your heart.
> Commit your way to the Lord;
> trust in him and he will do this. (Psalm 37:3–5)

There is a difference, however, between a whim and what we most *deeply desire*. Our growth along the path toward the heavenly places of identity in Christ includes a refinement of our desires. For example, there have been notable ministerial, educational, and even presidential people who have given themselves over to the desire for an affair with an intern or other colleague. I also have had many students and interns over the last thirty five years, but my deepest desires in those relationships were to be like Christ to them and to serve their growth in Christ. An affair would not have fulfilled my desire; it would have short-circuited my deepest desire and the friendships I now enjoy with many of those students. Ultimately our deepest desire and God's desire for us are identical; for he made us, gives us life, and our true identity is to be what he made us to be.

THE HEAVENLY PLACES

The character of Jesus Christ is the main quality of the heavenly places of our identity. When our character reflects the character of Jesus Christ, we are most true to ourselves: "If anyone is in Christ, then a new creation has come: The old has gone, the new is here!" (2 Cor. 5:17).There are four aspects of the character of Christ included in living out our identity as part of the new creation: *thought, perception, attitude,* and *stability*.

Thought

The quality of our *thought* affects all of our life as human beings and also as Christians. The cognitive-behavioral approach to psychotherapy places significant emphasis on *thought* as an aspect of depression and anxiety, their antidote in healthy living. Paul invites us in Romans to experience our lives in Christ through transformation of life "...by the renewing of your mind" (Rom. 12:2). Isaiah says that though our thoughts are not God's thoughts, his Word both expresses his thoughts and so accomplishes his purpose (see Isaiah 55:8–11).

Usually our thinking is either habitual, a knee-jerk reaction to a circumstance, or an attempt to figure out how we can get what we want or need in a given situation. The way we think, for example, about a chocolate chip cookie, or a financial need, or a neighbor, or one of our children will determine how we act toward that cookie, money, neighbor, or child.

Our identity in Christ involves thinking about life with the mind of Christ (see 1 Corinthians 2:16). Christ's thoughts in us can lead to gratitude for a couple of cookies (rather than gorging on a dozen!), work and budgeting for money, loving our neighbor as Christ would, and treating our child as God treats us.

Perception

There are a couple of aspects of our *thoughts* that are particularly important in living our identity in Christ: our *perception* of and our attitude toward people, places, and events. There was briefly a school of psychiatry that studied some mental illness as a visual defect. This effort was related to the frequency of visual hallucinations among some victims of mental illness. That effort was short-lived. But the spiritual significance of our perceptions was developed in tandem with logotherapy in a book by Bernard Tyrrell called *Christotherapy*.[2] The way we see our lives as new creations in Christ can inform and direct the character of Christ in us. We no longer *perceive* people as things, money as our possession, or chocolate chip cookies as tools to satisfy our lust; we see people as objects of God's love, money as a means to glorify and enjoy God, and chocolate chip cookies as gifts of God's creation to be received with moderation and gratitude.

Our attitude can grow toward a hope and joy-filled way of thinking about both the good and easy, but also the hard and challenging aspects of life. A positive attitude can contribute to stability of identity that is independent of the circumstances of our lives. One of my students from several years ago is a very good illustration of this stability of identity in Christ. She is the daughter of a professor at a Christian university that was surrounded by a quite erudite and affluent neighborhood. The family attended church and participated in social activities in that neighborhood where folks dressed, went on vacations, lived in houses, and generally enjoyed a lifestyle that was considerably beyond the means of others. This student was sensitive to the contrast between her lifestyle compared to her classmates and friends. And at times that was hard. But she was able for the most part to live a life of charm and grace in the heavenly places of her identity in Christ, knowing that in him she was clothed in the robes, wore the ring, and feasted at the feast of the King of Kings and Lord of Lords. She was a good example of what it looks like to live out our identity in Christ in the heavenly places.

THE QUESTIONS AND SCRIPTURES

1. How would you describe who you are in one paragraph? Write that down. (It may take a few days!)
2. How do you think God would describe his picture of who you are?
3. What are five cairns on the path you could follow to become more what God made you to be (for example, spend thirty minutes a day talking with your spouse, never take a bite of food you can't thank God for—that is, don't overindulge)?
4. What have you wanted deeply to do or be for God that you have avoided? What do you fear if you pursued your deepest desires? Do you need to talk to a friend, a pastor, or a counselor about your deepest desires and your identity?
5. What specific steps will you take this week to accomplish what you most deeply desire in Christ?
6. Scripture for further reflection: Ps. 139; John 3:1–17, 10:1–16; Gal. 2:20; 2 Cor. 5:11–21; 1 John 2:15–17, 3:1–3.

Chapter 4

PURPOSE: Why am I here?

My maternal grandfather committed suicide. He had made one previous attempt when my mother was twelve years old and afterward promised her that he would never leave her in that way. But when my mother was sixteen he went into the back yard, put a pistol to his head, and left her for the remainder of her earthly journey. She, and our family, lived with that legacy as a dark cloud, a constant reminder of the possibility that life can be deemed instantly as purposeless, to be buried six feet under. Of course we didn't talk about it much; it wasn't supposed to be mentioned in polite society. Only my father would bring it up, when he had to explain why mom would get so upset for no apparent reason.

Then, about thirty years later, my mother began to emerge from the darkness of that tragedy into the light of her heavenly Father. She began at first to read the Psalms, then Hannah Whithall Smith's book *The Christian's Secret of a Happy Life.*[1] She was affected by music, by the responsibilities of parenting her three children, and by studies of the Book of the Acts at a Bible college. And she began what became years of therapy with a pastoral counselor. She walked the path out of the darkest valley of her father's suicide, past the cairns of prayer, Bible, piano, parenting, and fellowship, into the heavenly places of a life of purpose, joy, and meaning.

Death can teach some of the hardest and most important lessons of life. The psalmist indicates this when he prays, "Teach us to number our days, that we may gain a heart of wisdom" (Ps. 90:12). And my maternal grandfather's death, though it was tragic, became a gift of life by prodding my mother to learn to live, and to live with purpose.

This legacy was in the back of my mind when, as a junior in high school, I read Thornton Wilder's play, *Our Town*.[2] The play takes place in Grover's Corners, New Hampshire about the turn of the nineteenth century, and focuses on the lives of Emily Webb and George Gibbs. They live seemingly uneventful, simple lives, get married, and then Emily dies giving birth to her first child. She is given the opportunity to revisit the earth from her grave, and chooses to return on her twelfth birthday. She carries on a conversation throughout the day with the stage manager, who serves as a grandfatherly God figure throughout the play. At one point she turns to him while she is invisibly observing the birthday preparations in her mother's kitchen and says, "It goes so fast. We don't have time to look at one another." Then, just before she returns to her grave she says goodbye to Grover's Corners and the life she has loved and known too little: "Good-by, Good-by, world. Good-by Grover's Corners …Mama and Papa. Good-by to clocks ticking…and Mama's sunflowers. And food and coffee. And new-ironed dresses and hot baths…and sleeping and waking up." And then she asks the stage manager, "Do any human beings ever realize life while they live it?—every, every minute?"[3]

That is the question of living life with purpose.

It is often a difficult question to answer, a challenging need to fulfill. The effect of my maternal grandfather's suicide on me was twofold: on the one hand I was dogged in my desire to discover my purpose for living; on the other hand I feared working as a minister in parish, because I knew I would need to counsel folks who questioned their reason to live. My own determination to live with purpose led to years of study, thought, journaling, seeing several psychotherapists, and hours of reflection on the book of Ecclesiastes. I began to realize that the purpose of each individual child of God is just that—individual, distinct for each person. I would agree with the Westminster Shorter Catechism: "The chief end of man is to glorify God and enjoy him forever."

There is also an individual purpose as well as a general end of humankind for the people of God. The Bible refers to this individual purpose as a calling for which we are given different gifts. (See 1 Corinthians 12:1ff and Ephesians 4:1ff) I realized that the call of God is fluid as

I studied further and reflected on the calling of folks I admire in my family, friends, ministers, and teachers. It is not rigid but develops along with the growth of life. A part of my calling was once to attend seminary and then graduate school to study marriage and family therapy. I am not called to do that anymore. My wife is not called to have children anymore; she is called these days to be the wonderful grandmother and wife she is. And sometimes the valleys in which we lose our sense of purpose result from rigid refusal to allow our calling to develop new dimensions over time. It is particularly depressing, sometimes to the point that life can seem to lose its purpose in old age, when our society insists that life is really worth living, every, every minute, only for folks in their twenties and thirties. God's purpose and calling do not leave us; God's Spirit grows our calling as life in Christ grows.

The other effect of my grandfather's death was my fear of serving those who through depression, loss, or biology questioned whether life was worth living. I had grown up with my mother's dreadful terror at the thought that somehow her father's death was her fault. And I had inherited a similar dread of failing those who need a sense of purpose and value in life. But over time I began to realize that people who have dealt with depression, even depression that includes suicidal thoughts, have the greatest capacity to develop a sense of positive purpose and joy. As a recovering alcoholic I had assumed most of my counseling practice would be with addiction issues. But instead I found myself focused in large part on supporting those who were developing a sense of purpose. For it is those who walk through the darkest valleys who can know life in the heavenly places of goodness, mercy, and abundance in the house of the Lord as long as we live (see Psalm 23). I came to realize over time that the deepest sense of purpose was not mine to give as a minister, counselor, or teacher; it is a gift of Jesus as the way, the truth, and the life.

The need for purpose is a need for significance. Gregory Bateson, one of the founders of the work of marriage and family therapy in the 1950s, spoke of "a difference that makes a difference."[4] His point was that there are some differences that are immaterial to the meaning and significance of life. It really doesn't make a lot of difference in the significance of our lives whether we speak German or English, whether we cut our fingernails daily or weekly, whether we are ten or thirty-three or seventy-two years old. Our lives can become a quagmire of failed solutions to the need for purpose when we live for things that don't matter.

My maternal grandmother, our Mimi, learned something from her husband's death: If the purpose of life is focused on things that don't matter, then the loss of those things can seem like the loss of our lives and can lead to suicidal thoughts about life. When I was a young boy, it used to make me mad when she said of a friend's slights or of the loss of a broken toy, "Honey, it doesn't really matter, does it?" I was too young to understand that underlying that question was an awareness of the importance of a purpose that could last, that was resilient against the losses of life.

THE VALLEYS

The Book of Ecclesiastes is the best description I know of the valley of meaninglessness, of purposelessness. The writer mentions virtually all of the failed answers we can devise to the question of why we are here, of the purpose of our lives. He chronicles the list of activities and pursuits that don't make a difference in giving a purposeful life: money, fame, pleasure, even things of value like friendship, religious observance, education, work, or morality. This is one of the most important books a person can study concerning our purpose because of its declaration that even the good things and activities in our lives are meaningless in themselves. The good things are indeed good, but if we build life around money or work or family or nation as the center of our purpose, we can starve our hearts and die of thirst in a valley of despair. A diminutive purpose is like living dietetically on water only, or only eating broccoli, or living by bread alone. It is not that the bread, broccoli, or water is bad; they are simply incomplete. Specifically, Ecclesiastes preaches that only a purpose that can live beyond death is meaningful.

It is only when the lives we live are centered in Jesus, *the* life, that *our* lives become purposeful. The writer of Ecclesiastes concludes that the only worthwhile purpose, in Old Testament terms, is to "Fear God and keep his commandments" (Eccles. 12:13). That, in New Testament terms, means to live life in Christ. It means coming to a point that we can say, with Paul, "to me, to live is Christ" (Phil. 1:21). Life centered in Christ is rich with purpose in all of its pleasure and pain and friendship and work. But without him, all the otherwise good stuff in our lives is loss. It's empty. Differences that make no difference. As Paul says, "I regard everything as loss because of the surpassing worth of knowing Christ Jesus my Lord" (Phil. 3:8).

There are two specific dimensions of the false purpose that have been particularly insidious in my life and the lives of those I have served: *idolatry* and *narcissism*.

Idolatry

It is no accident that the last verse of 1 John admonishes us, "Dear children, keep yourselves from idols" (1 John 5:21). Often when the Christian community hears a verse like that we think of all that's wrong with the world we live in. We hear that warning in terms of *others'* idolatry, not our own. But denial of idolatry can augment the power of that idolatry to drain and even destroy our lives, giving us false meaning and robbing us of our true purpose. And the idols that have tempted and robbed me have almost *all* been good things. Remember Ecclesiastes!

There is an example of which I am ashamed now but which illustrates the kind of idolatry I have seen in many students, church members, clients, and friends. It was a Saturday night many years ago when my ministry was increasingly important to me. I was still visiting church members long after my children had gone to bed. When I finally arrived home, my wife said one of those loving-yet-cutting truths that a good wife sometimes offers (though I sure didn't appreciate it at the time!). She said, "Honey, sometimes you seem to feel your ministry is more important than your family." I now can't believe my response; I said, "It is." She then asked me, with incredible love and gentleness, "Is your ministry also more important than God?" A long silence, then days of prayer followed. And I began to realize I had made an idol of ministry.

And with that realization, God was able to lead me, gently but firmly, up the path toward the heavenly places of *his* purpose for my life.

Obsessive-compulsive devotion of energy to someone or something is a symptom of the idolatry that can leave our lives malnourished at best, starving at worst. Obsessive and/or compulsive disorders rest on faith, faith that the object of our devotion can meet our need for significant life. But the address to obsessive-compulsive disorders, to use the psychobabble, must be made with tenderness and understanding. It has been said that a person can never raise a child, earn a medical degree, build a church, or accomplish any of a number of other worthwhile goals without a bit of obsessive-compulsion. For example, my wife crochets most of the Christmas gifts we give to family and friends each year. I sometimes complain that she seems to spend all her time crocheting! But the alternative would be spending big bucks and lots of time at malls and online shopping; in that light I have become right grateful for her fall crochet projects! The issue of obsessive-compulsion points to a distinction between idolatry and discipline. Discipline is pursuit of a goal with the energy, the power of the Spirit, focused on the good things of life for Christ's sake. Idolatry is pursuit of goals for their own sake.

Narcissism

Narcissism is the pursuit of all life for one's own sake. *Narcissism* is a fancy term for selfishness. It is as easy to attempt to correct selfishness by judgment as it is to correct idolatry by judgment. The problem with judgment of either idolatry or narcissism is that it's not effective. Narcissism, or selfishness, is an attempt to meet the human need for significance by gathering the people, events, work, goods, and kindred of our lives around ourselves.

Ecclesiastes shows that the very failure of both idolatry and narcissism to give us a lasting purpose can be a gift. Our failure to find purpose in the darkest valley can lead to a discovery of the path toward a purpose where our cup overflows.

THE PATHS

The path toward a purpose in the heavenly places passes by three primary cairns, three markers that God uses to give us his purpose and calling for our lives: *listening*, *vision*, and *relationship.*

Listening

The art of *listening* to our lives and to God's Word is largely lost in our society. Jesus says repeatedly throughout his teaching, "If anyone has ears to hear, let them hear" (Mark 4:23). One of the telltale signs of our absence of listening is the pace at which we both speak and absorb communications. Now I am quite aware of the fact that I grew up in Alabama and we talk *real* slow! But my goodness gracious, my wife and I have to watch news and other TV shows with the closed caption on, not because we're old and can't hear (though she says that's true of me when I want it to be!), but because the rate of words per minute is so incredibly fast among media folk. We all speak fast, think fast, drive fast, text fast, and listen fast.

We seem compelled to do life faster and faster. And Emily Webb was right; we don't take the time to look at or listen deeply to one another. During the Reformation period of church history, worship services lasted two hours and included a twenty-minute cantata; sermons lasted forty-five minutes to an hour! Any minister who preached a forty-five minute sermon these days would be fired on the spot, except perhaps in some African-American churches. I had the privilege of serving a predominantly African-American church during my parish work and I found there that people valued *listening*—deeply, long, with prayer and great emotion.

Our devotional time needs to be more than a one-page, five-minute reading if it is to yield an eventual sense of purpose and of God's call on our lives. In fact, in order to train our ears to really *listen,* we need to learn to live devotionally, to live with prayerful listening for God's Spirit as we move through life, not racing as if we're always trying to outrun God. Devotional living underlies the words of God to Joshua: "…you shall meditate…day and night" (Josh. 1:8, NKJV). Devotional living, living in constant listening for God, is also the root of Paul's word to the churches of Rome: "…be transformed by the renewing of your mind…" (Rom. 12:2). This constant listening for and living in Christ can be illustrated by the way we think in traffic; just contrast the words you usually say to yourself if someone cuts you off in traffic and the words you might say if you were carrying on a conversation with Jesus sitting in the passenger seat. Get the picture?

The simple key words of this book (like hope, love, pleasure, purpose, pain, and identity) have occupied years of listening over my seventy years. I can see that one legacy of my maternal grandfather's tragic death is a gift, my gift of hunger to discover the wonder, the beauty, the purpose of this wonderful life God gives us. And such a discovery requires careful, slow, protracted *listening* to God, to ourselves, and to Jesus, the life. It is ironic that I learned to listen from my other paternal grandfather. He would often sit on his porch swing, swatting flies, and I would ask, "What you doing, granddad?" He would usually reply, "Just chasin' a thought down to its end, son." I would ask again, "Where does the thought end, granddad?" And he would say, with a sparkle in those Welsh blue eyes, "All good thoughts begin and end with God, son. So I'm just travelin' from God at the beginning of my thoughts back to God at the end of my thoughts." And I'd think about that.

Vision

If we learn to listen to God, to ourselves, and to life, we can come to a *vision* of our purpose in life. Such a vision may be assisted by a test for the discovery of our spiritual gifts or a book like Rick Warren's *Purpose Driven Life*.[5] But a test or book alone cannot give us a sense of purpose with the resilience to stand up to all life can throw at us.

That became apparent in the life of a young lady who endured a horrendous experience at the hands of a man in Atlanta who had committed a crime and took refuge in this lady's apartment. Her life had been, like most of our lives at one time, confused and devoid of meaning and purpose. But she had been reading Warren's book not long before she was held hostage during those agonizing hours. She read part of the book to her hostage-taker, prayed for him, and suggested some of the possibilities God might have for his life. But the book did not deliver her from the hostage situation by itself. She was *listening* to God in that situation and seeing the *vision* of God's presence and purpose. The book gave her the glasses to assist her; but God gave her the *vision*.

Relationship

The ultimate cairn which we dare not miss on our path to the heavenly places of purposeful living is a *relationship* with God, with Jesus the way, the truth, and the life. All the abilities, the accomplishments, and the functions around which we build our lives, can vanish in an instant. But if our *relationship* with God becomes the focal purpose of our lives and occupies the center of all the various activities to which we are called, our lives become eternal. As 1 John says, "The world and its desires pass away, but whoever does the will of God lives forever" (1 John 2:17).There is a devotional reflection by Oswald Chambers that my wife shared with me and which get at this centrality of our relational purpose for living in Christ: "The purpose of my life belongs to God, not me."[6] We may have many, quite diverse, callings, but we have only one purpose: "Follow me" (John 21:19). When we become focused on life with Jesus, that relationship can fill us with an eternal reason for being here, "every, every minute."

THE HEAVENLY PLACES

There is never a time when God's purpose is perfectly realized in us; but there is also never a time when God's love is not reaching out to draw us to himself and his purpose to live in intimacy with us. This life can include the summit of living in the *focus*, the *confidence*, and the *gratitude* that characterize the heavenly places of God's purpose.

Focus

Jesus shows what it looks like to live life in the heavenly places of God's purpose. He did not become shortsighted as we are prone to do; he did not *focus* only on one of the activities, services, or missions he was called to. He came to live as one with his father; he invites us to live as one with him (see John 14–17). He was not focused on teaching, healing, dying, rising, or doing miracles; he was focused on living out his life in unity with his father; and out of that relationship he taught, healed, died, rose again, and did miracles. The first characteristic of a Christian life of purpose is *focus* on our relationship with God. The parenting, preaching, business, athletics, play, service, prayer, or Sunday School teaching we may be called to do is ultimately just a reflection of that relationship.

There are two statements that express this *focus* on our relationship with God: first, "With God all things are possible" (Matt. 19:26), and second, "Apart from me you can do nothing" (John 15:5).

Confidence

A second characteristic of a purposeful life in Christ is *confidence*. This has been a difficult area for me when I have felt that my calling was too big for me, that it depended on me, and that I would get a bad grade. My childhood seemed to teach me that I was inadequate and prone to failure. Once in elementary school I got in trouble for not paying attention in class and was sent to the principal's office. He said, "Madoc, I don't understand; both your parents are college professors and you should be one of our brightest and best students." He didn't realize that he had just expressed precisely why I did poorly in school; I felt I could never measure up to my parents. It was an incredible relief when I began to move toward God's purpose; all I had to do was live in relationship with Jesus, the way, the truth, and the life. All else would flow from that simple, powerful relationship.

Gratitude

The third quality of life in the heavenly places of God's purpose is the opposite of what my maternal grandfather demonstrated in his suicide: Life in God's purpose is life in *gratitude*. This book does not shy away from the difficulties of life; in fact it was written to show some ways forward to joy and gladness out of those difficulties. But as difficult as life can be, there is in Christ no day in which we cannot live with great gratitude if those lives are focused on the purpose of God to live in relationship with him. Every morning, every breath, every flower, path, job, smile, tear, touch, every clock ticking, freshly ironed dress, hot bath, and every time we lie down to sleep can be a time of gratitude if it is lived in the purpose of loving and living Christ.

THE QUESTIONS AND SCRIPTURES

1. What are you living for (Write this in a journal or someplace you can look at later; this may take a long time; it took me years)?
2. How has your purpose for life been challenged and how have you met those challenges?
3. What part(s) of your purpose are transient (for example winning a race or competition, owning a house, raising a family, getting a job)?
4. What is Christ's purpose in loving you? What is he after in his love for you? What does he want to see happen in your life?
5. What are three specific things you could do to correlate Christ's purpose in loving you and your purpose in living (for example, get a counseling appointment to deal with a blow to your reason for living, follow Christ by letting go of smoking, thank God for at least fifteen small gifts each day)?
6. Scripture for further reflection: Josh. 1:1–8; Ps. 1, 90; Eccl. 1:1–11, 12:9–14; Rom. 12:1–21; Phil. 1:12–26, 3:7–14.

Chapter 5

GRACE: How can I live fully?

This man wanted to destroy the church. He saw Christianity as a cult, an aberration of all that was holy, just, and good. He thought Christians blasphemously challenged the traditions and the law, in spite of Jesus' saying he came to fulfill the law. In fact, this man's background, education, birthright, and religious patriotism taught him that if the followers of Jesus were allowed to continue, it could spell the end of God's purpose for humankind. And he had the elite social standing and the wealth to make his convictions felt far and wide throughout the Christian world. So at the hands of this man, people were being falsely accused and prosecuted to the full extent of the law, sentenced to severe punishment, and some killed. But among those with whom he had grown up, he was a star. He had many followers who participated in his "holy war" against the church. He was, for his day, a near-perfect model terrorist.

When I was a young pastor, I had a Rembrandt print of him on the wall. For his terrorism toward the church was not the whole story.

His name was Saul of Tarsus, and he became known as the apostle Paul. (The apostle Paul actually had two names, which was common among Hellenistic Jews in the first century. He is referred to as Saul until Acts 13:9, after which he is called Paul.) Jesus brought the old Saul of Tarsus out of the life he had known, then raised Paul to a new life. The apostle Paul became the single most outstanding champion of the gospel of grace in the early church. He had done all he could to earn God's favor and acceptance under the law, but on the road to Damascus Paul saw his abject failure, he saw all of us failing, to earn God's approval. Paul became a recipient of grace, the good news that God gives his favor, compassion, and acceptance without price, without merit, solely by his unconditional loving will to bring us alive through Jesus Christ.

Jesus' appearance ripped apart Paul's entire world; that voice from heaven threw him to the ground, then lifted him up a new man. The conversion on the road to Damascus is a picture of the grace of God and the revolution, destruction, and new creation that occurs when grace happens. But Jesus' message was so unsettling that Paul had to get away.

We don't know exactly how long he spent in Arabia. We read that after his baptism he "went away at into Arabia, and returned again to Damascus" (Gal. 1:17, ESV).The consensus of most scholars is that Paul went to the region around either Mount Sinai or Mount Hebron to rethink his faith after his conversion. The autobiographical aspects of Philippians 3 indicate that Paul would spend the rest of his life learning a new way of living; he now saw his old life as "loss because of the surpassing worth of knowing Christ Jesus my Lord" (Phil. 3:7, ESV). The grace of God rearranged Paul's way of trying to live fully. And, understandably, it took some time for Paul to absorb what God was doing in him and how he would think, work, and live from that point on.

"How can I live fully?" That is the question Paul had to answer as he reexamined the motives, the means, the very purpose of his existence after meeting Jesus. That is the question that underlies every other question in this book. It is the question I had after becoming consistently sober. It is the question my wife had after brain surgery. It is the question I had when I first jumped in the Coosa River in water over my head and wondered if I knew enough about swimming to survive. It's the question every mother has at the birth of her first child. "How can I live fully?"

It is the question that arises from the simplest yet most fundamental need we have as human beings: the need to find a way to really come alive. It is the question I experienced when I was asked at my ordination examination if I had any hesitation about becoming an ordained United Methodist minister. I answered that if I were not anxious about my inadequacy to fulfill the call of God, I would question whether I *was* called of God. Then I quoted Paul: "Not that we are competent in ourselves…" (2 Cor. 3:5). Then I said I do not fear what may happen as long as I find my sufficiency through God's grace. Instead I fear the tendency all of us have to *avoid* life by grace and to attempt to live life and service out of my own strength, education, ingenuity, and willpower.

Jesus says, "I am the way and the truth and the life" (John 14:6). That is the promise that God gives us life through faith alone, by grace alone.

THE VALLEYS

Grace looks easy. But the ascent from the valleys surrounding the heavenly places of grace is a challenging and sometimes unpleasant climb. Clients, church members, and I have had difficulty understanding, accepting, and living by grace.

Most of us, like Saul of Tarsus before his conversion, believe in justice or fairness. We believe that we should receive an honest day's wage for an honest day's work. We believe that in marriage there should be fair exchanges of give and take. We believe that good things should happen to good people, and bad things should only happen to bad people. We also believe that if we can be good enough or powerful enough that we can *make* good things happen in our lives. We even come to believe that we can force God to be good to us. We are, after all, entitled to his goodness if we do the best we can to please him. Aren't we?

If that seems a bit harsh, think of Job. For the problem of Job is the problem of each of us. We, like Job in his complaint against God, and Paul before his conversion, believe we can earn and achieve life on our own willpower, goodness, and resources. We are entitled to a good life, and if we don't get it, if life is harsh with us, we blame God. We even, like Job, judge God.

This belief in earned entitlement is the glacier that digs a valley—a valley that imprisons human life in a desperate frenzy to prove we can do life on our own. There are three sources that feed this glacier: *legalism, power,* and *pride*. It is important to point out at the outset that each of us walks on this glacier. Each of us is subject to its crevasses and dangers.

Resistance to grace is subtle, however. It doesn't look problematic like alcoholism or immoral pursuit of pleasure or stealing. It is an attitude that can infect our whole lives and yet leave our whole lives looking very good and very Christian. In fact, there are many churches that are led by pastors, elders, teachers, and others who do the good in their lives not *because* of God's favor, but to *earn* God's favor. Their appearance of rectitude and goodness is the reason Jesus warned of their presence as tares, noxious weeds among the wheat of his kingdom (see Matthew 13:24–30, NKJV).

Legalism

One of the greatest threats to Christianity in the first century was *legalism,* or adherence to the law as a source of righteousness. The term is not used in the Bible, but the principle is universal. The heart of legalism is the belief that salvation, blessing, or a good life is earned and becomes an entitlement resulting from compliance with an external standard such as the Ten Commandments. It is a mercenary Christianity in which we believe God owes us the payment of his acceptance because of the good we have done. This was (and is) considered such a threat to Christianity because it undermines the gift of God's grace. Paul, especially in Galatians, makes a clear distinction between a relationship with God based on grace and one based on earnings.

This desire to earn life, blessing, and the approval of God is intense and tenacious. If we earn it, it is our possession, our claim upon God. He owes us because we are so good and others are so bad. If our life and relationship with God is our right by obedience to the law, we control it. One of the most frequently tantalizing comments by sportscasters as we move toward playoff and championship season is that a team "controls its own destiny." Doesn't that sound good to our ears? We so yearn to live in control of our sport, our marriage, our salvation, or even our God himself.

The problem in the New Testament, and in our lives, is not so much that we want to live completely by the law; we just want to finish up that way. Paul chides the Galatian Christians for thinking they can begin by grace and then, after a good jump start from God's Spirit, they virtually say, "We can take it from there, thank you very much" (see Galatians 3:3). It's as if we believe all we need is to be forgiven for the past and then we can at least be good enough that we'll deserve God's blessings from that point on.

We become trapped in the dark valley of anxious clamoring after the right to God's approval. And that is a slap in the face of God. For he gave all he had to love us into life, knowing that we could never earn that love, and that if we tried our lives would be spent in constant fear of the sin that lies so close at hand for all of us. Or as Hebrews says even more strongly of those who resist grace: "they crucify again for themselves the Son of God, and put him to an open shame" (Heb. 6:6, NKJV).

Power

Power is a most deceptive force against life by grace. Power can lead us to believe that the weak may need grace for God's approval and blessing, but if we are big enough, strong enough, rich enough, and important enough, surely God is obligated to love us, bless us, and give us the good life to which we have a right. Lord Acton was not just talking about political dynamics when he said, "Power tends to corrupt, and absolute power corrupts absolutely."[1] This is what Jesus said definitively: "It is hard for a rich man to enter the kingdom of heaven" (Matt. 19:23, NKJV). It is not just the power of wealth that obstructs acceptance of grace. Other sources of power like education, ethnicity, athletic ability, religiously significant position, or a good family can also build up a resistance to the need for grace.

It is not, of course, that anyone in their right mind really believes that their power can force God's approval or compel life to be good. But power is deceptive. If a person has enough financial, political, interpersonal, social, or in some cases ecclesiastical power, their position can lure them into believing that grace is for the other fellow, not for them. Jesus says to the powerful, "You say, 'I am rich; I have acquired wealth and do not need a thing.' But you do not realize that you are wretched, pitiful, poor, blind and naked" (Rev. 3:17).

Pride

Now we get to the heart of the matter. The reason *legalism* is so tenacious and *power* so deceptive is that we really want to be the god of our own lives. Sounds kind of dumb, doesn't it? Yet *pride* is the disease, the dysfunction that infects each of us with sinful resistance to grace. For our life is not our own if we live from, by, and for the grace of God in Jesus

Christ. We belong to the God who has given his life that we might receive our lives as a gift. It is no longer my life of which I am god, but "The life which I now live in the body, I live by faith in the Son of God, who loved me and gave himself for me" (Gal. 2:20).

Our very existence in grace is a daily testimony that we are dependent on, and live out our lives in need of and dependence on God's love, power, purpose, and direction. We are not our own man, not our own woman, although grace itself brings an authentic sense of self beyond any self-created life, as we will see further in the "Heavenly Places" part of this chapter.

When I was a senior at Indian Springs High School, just south of Birmingham, Alabama, I wrote a paper comparing two essays written around the same period of history. One was Ralph Waldo Emerson's essay, "On Self-Reliance." The other was Jonathan Edwards' essay, "God Glorified by Man's Dependence." Emerson's goal, along with transcendentalist philosophers in general, was individual freedom and integrity. But I concluded in that paper that a life by grace or, in Edwards' terms, life in dependence on God, brings more individual integrity and freedom from oppression than the self-defined and self-reliant life Emerson advocated. That conclusion has been confirmed and expanded many times over in my life since those teen years.

THE PATHS

There are three primary cairns marking the path toward life by grace. These are the *authorization* to live, the *strength* to live, and the *direction* of life. Another translation of the biblical words underlying these cairns is justification, power, and guidance. These cairns are really quite familiar to all of us in common parlance. They relate to the permission for, the ability to engage in, and the behavior connected with happiness. These cairns mark the heart of the climb toward fulfilled life in Christ. They reflect the kinds of questions that might seem silly on the surface but actually are fundamental to human life and Christian fulfillment: Is it OK for me to have good life? Am I able to have good life? What do I do, what really happens in good life?

Authorization

"Am I *authorized* to live?" is a question about the justification of or permission to be happy, to really live. It's the question on the face of one of our sons on a day that I'll never forget. He stood in the kitchen with one of my wife's chocolate chip cookies (which I, to this day, think came directly from the heavenly places of culinary delight!) and he said by his expression, "Daddy, is it OK if I have this cookie?"

The message of the grace of God in the cross of Jesus Christ is that you are wanted. It is not only permissible for you to have the chocolate chip cookie, the calling, the motherhood, the home, and the joys of your life. God wanted that for you so much that he rejected himself in the person of his own Son that he might have you and that you might have life!

This was a major issue for a client, now deceased, who grew up with a sense that his parents, his father especially, did not want him; he was just one more mouth to feed. And when he was eleven years old, he was taken to a mountain near his house, told he was on his own, and he never saw his mother or father again. He wondered ferociously, even after years of the healing work of God's grace, "Is it OK? Am I *authorized* to have a happy life with a wife and children? Or am I a piece of trash to be thrown in the garbage can of life?"

The parable of the treasure hidden in the field (Matt. 13:44) has always spoken powerfully to me. In some ways, it is a parable about giving priority to being part of the kingdom of God. But many years ago, Lloyd Ogilvie gave his readers a gift by excavating a deeper truth out of that parable.[2] It is not just that God wants us to seek the kingdom of God above all else. It is also that he, by this grace we so desire and need, gave all he had that he might have *us*, that he might bring *us,* that he might save *us* to be a part of his family.

You are *authorized,* by the loving blood and gracious Spirit of our God, to live, and to live fully. There are two biblical words that convey this decree that God wills our life abundant. The word in the letters of Paul is "justification." Paul writes:

> There is no difference between Jew and Gentile, for all have

> sinned and fall short of the glory of God, and all are justified freely by his grace through the redemption that came by Jesus Christ. (Rom. 3:22–24)

The term "justified" is often perceived as a word of forensic declaration, which it is. But God's declaration that we are righteous in Jesus Christ also has a powerful psychological message: "You are authorized to live, and to live fully."

I used to be puzzled by one of the words in the prologue to John's Gospel, which is filled with gospel wealth. God gives us, according to John 1:12, the "right" to become the children of God. The word "right," which is translated in various ways, derives from a verb that refers to giving permission. Do you hear the good news? God gives you permission or authorization to live; He says it's fine and dandy for you to be a child of the King of Kings and Lord of Lords. It's OK for you to have good life! God says so! Life by grace keeps this giant cairn of God's grace ever in view, to keep us on the path toward life.

Strength

An eighteen-year-old young man can easily see himself as ten feet tall and bulletproof. There were times when it was my turn to lead our cross-country team in roving through the hills and woods south of Birmingham, Alabama that I pretty well acted as if I were invincible, strong as a young bull. But I knew better. When the first light of the sunrise of Jesus Christ began to shine in my life, my weakness attracted me to Philippians 4:13: "I can do all things through Christ who strengthens me" (NKJV).

But I wondered just how that strengthening might happen. I still wonder sometimes.

I have discovered that four factors are always present when God's grace brings the strength we need to have a good and full life: prayer, supportive community, sacramental dependence on God, and the reception of God's Word.

Prayer is a source of strength *not* because it is a means of getting a list of good stuff from God. It is not meant to be a resource only for Christmas presents and parking places. Prayer is the conscious absorption of God into every nook and cranny of our lives. Robert Boyd Munger's booklet, *My Heart—Christ's Home*, has been one of my favorite pieces of Christian literature for many years.[3] That well-loved piece describes in eloquent simplicity the process of God's Spirit entering and occupying each room of our heart: our study, living areas, eating, storage areas, bedroom, and recreational lives. It is a beautiful description of a life of prayer, of receiving Christ not only as Savior and Lord but as a friend, companion, and transformer of what may be at times drab and uninteresting aspects of life into a glorious habitation of God. The Living Bible paraphrases 2 Corinthians 12:9 to express the strength that comes from simply living in Christ's presence: "I am with you; that is all you need."

Let's be specific. We are so accustomed to thinking of prayer as delivering a list of requests to God that we miss this strengthening that comes from absorbing God's presence. And making requests is a fine form of prayer. This, for example, would be a splendid prayer: "Dear God, I pray you will be with all those I love and this nation and help us all to live in your will and grow in your grace. Be especially with Aunt Ruby and our son Jimmy, and please help our cat Samson to have your comfort as he deals with his old age. In Jesus' Name, Amen."

There is another kind of prayer that might go something like this: "Wow, Lord, what a pleasure to wake up with you. I still remember what it was like to wake up during the drinking days—hung over, lonely, and scared. Thank you for sobriety this morning. And thank you for my wife—she probably thinks I'm still asleep and she's getting coffee and doing devotions in the kitchen. Thank you we have each other yet another day. Direct the words I write today, I pray, and even more direct my heart as I write. Grant, Lord, that the words will be real, and will help. Boy do I ever thank you for the smell of fresh coffee. And for our dogs. And for the liver transplant. It's kind of hard, Lord, to keep exercising when I can't do what I used to do during the climbing days; help me to remember to enjoy the fact that I still can exercise a bit, even if I ain't quite the lean, mean climbin' machine I once was. Lord, you really are fun. Let's keep this conversation going today. Time for coffee. . . ." That is the prayer that started my day this morning. It was a funnel through which God poured the strength of his grace into life today.

And God's Word does the same. That Word can come through preaching, rereading a booklet, or comparing translations of a verse. But God's Word never comes without protracted, quiet, repetitive thought. The Bible calls that meditation. I'm not an aficionado of yoga, but I'm told that yoga along with mental repetition of God's Word can be a fine way to absorb the Spirit's perspectives on life. My dad found walking with the sounds of classical music in his earphones aided his meditation on the things of God. Mom had her prayer and meditation chair that she kept with her till the last of her earthly days. I had a minister as a young man who compared meditation to a cow chewing its cud; rather earthy, but I think of that illustration often as I roll a passage around in my soul. One of my sons gave me a gift for my seventieth birthday that I find a really good aid to meditation; *The 17:18 Series* gives an opportunity to write the words of Scripture by hand and make notes on what is written.[4] Another son writes quotes from Christian writers like C.S. Lewis, Bonhoeffer, Milton, Augustine, and others four or five times a week on Facebook. The form of meditation doesn't matter; the practice of meditation matters a great deal. For absorbing the Word of God through meditation gives the strength of his grace.

Direction

Backpackers who meet on the trail often ask, if they stop to speak and sip some water, "Where you goin'?" It's one of those simple yet very significant questions. Many of us have spent at least some time perhaps wandering around Europe or driving around on a Sunday afternoon like a vagabond. But eventually life by grace becomes life with direction.

God guides people who are in motion. This point is ably spelled out by Lloyd Ogilvie in his little book, *God's Will in Your Life*.[5] He points out that a sailboat that is "in irons," or in a period with no wind whatsoever, is for all practical purposes rudderless; it cannot be guided. There is a parallel principle at work in one of the sayings in Alcoholics Anonymous; when you don't know what to do, "Do the next right thing." If a Christian doesn't know what to do next in his or her life, obedience to what we do know to do, in terms of exercise, service, giving, and loving those around us can give God a person in motion whom he can guide.

There are times in the life of any pastor when the next steps in parish work can seem muddled, cloudy at best. I had some of those times as a younger man in my first church appointment in Melvin, Alabama. Now, Melvin is not exactly a big place; at the time I served the Melvin United Methodist Church (and two other churches, to fill out the work week) there were 110 registered voters. I wondered, after I spent my twenty hours of sermon study and necessary programing, what I was to do next. Well, I would play some catch with one of our sons, and hoe in the garden, then barbeque some chicken. Then what?

When I occasionally became depressed with a sense that I wasn't accomplishing much, I would do the one thing I knew would help someone. I would visit folks. And after a thorough discussion about the weather and the deer hunting that year, we would talk about Jesus. One visit at a time, one sermon at a time, and then one child's birth at a time, God wove together four of the best years of our lives. We were directed, by God's grace, simply to love each other and the people of Melvin, Alabama. And it was wonderful.

THE HEAVENLY PLACES

Grace looks easy. But the ascent from the valleys surrounding the heavenly places of grace is a challenging, sometimes tough climb. Clients, church members, and I have had difficulty understanding, accepting, and living by grace. Those words introduced the outline of the valleys preceding grace; they also introduce the heavenly places to which grace leads.

Life in grace is life in a realm so different from the usual way of doing things that both its beginning and its endpoint can feel difficult. Grace is at the heart of Jesus' statement to Pilate: "My kingdom is not of this world." The heavenly places of grace are not of this world, either. These places include both *freedom* and combined *humility and exaltation.*

Humility and Exaltation

There are many paradoxical, seemingly contradictory, elements of Christian life, which are wonderfully combined in Christ. If you are crucified with Christ, you can have the fullness of the risen life of Christ (see Galatians 2:20). If you lose your life in Christ, you can find your true life saved (see Matthew 16:25–26). If you humble yourself, you will be exalted to a position above the values and attitudes of this world (see Luke 14:11, 18:14). James quotes from Proverbs, "God…gives grace to the humble" (James 4:6, NKJV). The combination of *humility* and a life that is *exalted* above anything the world has to offer is the paradox of the heavenly places of grace.

The humility that the Bible encourages is a far cry from self-rejection or self-hatred. The Latin term for humility derives from a word relating to the fertility of soil. The humility of the Bible is a receptive fertility that is eager to receive, nurture, and bring fruition to the Word of God. It is a willingness to let God be God rather than living life out of either our own devices or the approval or lordship of others. The humility of the Bible is a willingness to walk beside Jesus on the trail to the heavenly places, following the cairns, the trail markers he has placed rather than wandering around with the attitude that we know better how to climb than Jesus "…the pioneer and perfecter of faith" (Heb. 12:2).

Christians run like scolded dogs from the idea of superiority to others, or *exaltation,* in an absolute terror of appearing "holier than thou." I personally felt at one time that the passages dealing with separation from or avoiding love for the world were a bit "over the top" (see, for example, 1 John 2:15–17 and 2 Corinthians 6:17). Then I listened to my wife and her insights from Al-Anon concerning detachment. Later I began to learn from clients, students, and church members that some relationships and environments are toxic in a variety of ways, especially spiritually. Gradually I began to learn that a Christian can both stand above, be *exalted* above, the proud who consider themselves beyond the need for grace and at the same time love them. I learned from my wife and others I served that a Christian can both detach from toxic influences while having compassion for those who are mired in that toxicity.

Jesus achieved that combination of humility and exaltation, blended together in love, in his stance toward the Pharisees. He was at times sharp, some would even say divisive, toward them (see Matthew 23). But most of the time Jesus treated proud pharisaical resistance to grace with compassion and occasionally a bit of humorous "reverse snobbery."

An example of the compassion follows his diatribe against the self-righteous pride of the Pharisees and Sadducees in Matthew 23: "Jerusalem, Jerusalem…how often I have longed to gather your children together… and you were not willing" (Matt. 23:37). His humorous confrontation of self-righteous judgment flows throughout his ministry. He says, for example, "Why do you look at the speck of sawdust in your brother's eye and pay no attention to the plank in your own eye?" (Matt. 7:3). Picture that and you'll smile. Jesus' invitation to combine humility and exaltation to the superiority of walking with him was both powerful and winsome. And it results in the *freedom* for which we all yearn.

Freedom

Freedom is the abundant life of God's grace (see John 10:10). And freedom is always a relative term; it is a term of motion from that which binds and toward that which fulfills. It is both freedom *from* and freedom *for*. It is freedom from death and for life; it is freedom from sin and for righteousness; it is freedom from addiction and for sobriety; it is freedom from cancer and for courage; it is freedom from all the fears and obstacles to a life of good; it is freedom for the glory and enjoyment of God.

Freedom, although it is one of the hallmarks of American history and of the desires of humankind throughout history, is both a profound human need and one of the most significant deprivations in our society. We are deprived of freedom to the extent that we are bound by the prison of our own proud disdain for grace.

Paul proclaims, as he begins to conclude his epistle of grace to the churches of Galatia, "It is for freedom that Christ has set us free" (Gal. 5:1). The freedom that is ours in the grace of God is liberation from all the sin, dysfunction, and deprivation of each of the valleys of the shadow of death in this book. And this freedom is the energizing, empowering invitation of God to join him in a romp through the meadows and summits of each of the heavenly places of *Climbing Home*, and beyond all the meadows and up to the summits of this life. Freedom in Christ is God's breathing into us again the breath of life and saying, as he did to the dry, dead bones of Ezekiel, "I will make breath enter you, and you will come to life.… Then you will know that I am the Lord" (Ezek. 37:5–6). The freedom of the grace of God in Jesus Christ invites us, this Word of God resounding through the Cross, shining across history in the Lord of the resurrection, reverberating in our hearts by the Holy Spirit:

> Ho! Everyone who thirsts,
> Come to the waters;
> And you who have no money,
> Come, buy and eat.
> Yes, come buy wine and milk
> Without money and without price.
> Why do you spend money for what is not bread,
> And your wages for what does not satisfy?
> Listen carefully to me, and eat what is good.
> And let your soul delight itself in abundance. (Isa. 55:1–2, NKJV)

Now that…that is the freedom and joy of grace!

THE QUESTIONS AND SCRIPTURES

1. What do you rely on the most for your major life choices? For your small, daily choices (for example, mom's opinion, prayer, counseling, devotions)?
2. What gives you strength (for example, music, exercise, journaling)?
3. What are five of the people, events, or attitudes that leave you feeling most disqualified to receive good in your life (for example, my boss, a traumatic event, addiction)? What does God say about those five influences? What can you do about the toxic influences in your life?
4. What are five of the people, events, or attitudes that leave you feeling most authorized to receive good in your life (for example, grandmother, church, date night)? How could you cultivate those influences of grace?
5. What is the primary area of your life where you need more freedom? What could you do to get it? When will you do that?

6. What are the three passages that convey to you the grace of God? (For me, these would include Isaiah 63, Psalm 37, John 10, 14–16, Ephesians 1, Philippians 3–4.) How often do you think about those passages?
7. Write out those passages that convey God's grace to you. What do those passages lead you to do? When will you do it?
8. Scripture for further reflection: Ps. 51; Hosea 11:1–11; Zeph. 3:9–20; Matt. 20:1–16; Rom. 6:1–14; Gal. 2:19–3:29.

Part II
Questions of Love

"The Lord God said, 'It is not good for the man to be alone'" (Gen. 2:4). That was well before sin entered the picture. God designed the creation to be an expression of his identity, and that would not be possible if humankind lived in isolation. For God himself lives in eternal relationship as Father, Son, and Holy Spirit.

One of the most significant contributions of the Swiss theologian and pastor, Karl Barth, to the Christian community was his exegesis of this verse: "So God created mankind in his own image, in the image of God he created them; male and female he created them" (Gen. 1:27). Following the grammatical rules of Hebrew parallelism, he says that life in the image of God is life as male and female in relationship.[1] A life lived in isolation from others is not human life as God made it.

God created attraction as a nurturing stimulus of human life in relationship. Hormonal and other sources of attraction did not just drop out of the sky. If we believe in God as creator in any form, with or without evolution, we are led by Scripture to believe that his will included the attraction that leads to committed relationships, and is one of the stimuli that leads a man to marry his wife.

Life in relationship also includes a gravitational pull toward community among both men and women. Men are drawn to other men who can help to form a community of protection and provision for wives and families. These communities are structured as armies, nations, churches, states, tribes, and are reflected even in sports teams. Women are attracted to other women who can form communities that help with the process of homemaking and child-rearing. These are structured as prayer groups, sororities, women's associations and ministries, and social missions such as Mothers Against Drunk Driving. These relationships beyond marriage take the form of the fellowship or friendship of God's people (see for example 1 John 1; John 15), and these structures of marriage, fellowship, and friendship take place largely in family and church.

These primal attractions and relationship structures are the foundation of human community. Paul says, "And now these three remain: faith, hope, and love. But the greatest of these is love" (1 Cor. 13:13). The greatest is love not because of some romantic or sentimental notion that love is so sweet; love is the hallmark of Christian life because it most reflects the internal relationship and nature of God. Love is the greatest quality among the people of God because "God is love" (1 John 4:16). We love God, life, ourselves, and others "because he first loved us" (1 John 4:19). The beginning of that love for us and among us was God's correction of the only thing he considered "not good" in creation before the fall: the isolation of the man he had created.

The next five chapters are designed to put shoe leather to our understanding and practice of love. They are also designed to outline some of the ways in which love feeds faith and leads to hope. It is common to say love is not only an emotion. These chapters are designed to describe in practical terms the distortions of love that plague our relationship valleys of despair, the path toward living in love as God loves us (see Ephesians 5:2), and the life in love that characterizes the heavenly places of love we hope for and can come to know in Christ.

CHAPTER 6

LOVE: WILL I BE ALONE?

I knew, I just knew for sure that if I went into that school for the first day of first grade, I would be left alone for the rest of my life. I grabbed one of the poles outside Woodrow Wilson Elementary and it took four teachers to pry me loose from my last defense against a powerful fear of abandonment. I later agreed to go to school only if my mother promised to drive by at least five times during the day. And I would watch for her, hoping to gain some reassurance that I was not left alone in the world. I later spent years in therapy trying to understand and resolve this fear.

My desperation for relationship took many dysfunctional turns. Only after years of groveling in dark relationship valleys did I understand that pursuing every attraction that comes down the pike is not love. I was so terribly afraid of abandonment that I chased after any and all attractions and destroyed many relationships in the process. I anesthetized my fear of abandonment with alcohol, sought after the relationship that might finally save me, and lost my soul. I became divorced. I became alcoholic. I became lost, lost to my family, to myself, and to God.

But Jesus loves "to seek and to save the lost" (Luke 19:10). God began to rebuild my life. He made it clear that I could not start from some point in the past before I had acquired the scrapes and scars of my tormented years. God does not take us back to a point of supposed innocence; he takes us forward from today. God said to me, through the mouth of a prophet who himself had known dark valleys,

> Because of the Lord's great love, we are not consumed,
>   for his compassions never fail.
> They are new every morning;
>   great is your faithfulness. (Lam. 3:22–23)

And so I began to pursue healing. One step at a time, as my mother had prayed so often, God did his work of restoring the years that the locust of feared abandonment had consumed (see Joel 2:25). I began to work. I began the journey toward sobriety. I began therapy. God breathed into the dry bones of my ravaged soul the breath of life. I began to live again. And he said, as he had at my beginning, "It is not good for the man to be alone" (Gen. 2:18). He restored my soul, and then he restored my life in a healthy, godly relationship. I was married.

Few of my early therapists ever suggested that my fear of abandonment was at least partly a primal instinct rooted in creation itself. There were many wonderful, life-changing hours spent in those psychotherapists' offices; and some of them influence me still. But it was especially a therapist, in Mobile, Alabama, who gently walked with me toward a productive path.

I began to realize that my fear of abandonment did not need to be eliminated as much as it needed to be replaced by a sense that I had been, was, and would be loved and wanted. My therapist helped me absorb the presence, love, and grace of a God who said "Never will I leave you; never will I forsake you" (Heb. 13:5). And she helped me realize that my wife was a part of God's faithful presence in my life. My fear of abandonment began to subside and to be replaced by the joy of love in Christ and my marriage. I became, over time, as God intended, not alone.

There was a long path ahead of me. But I had begun a process of receiving the love of God that became the core of my life and the core of this book. I had begun *Climbing Home*.

THE VALLEYS

The greatest evils occur in realms that God designed for the greatest good. The most wonderful gifts of God can become the most destructive idols. It is precisely in the sphere of the image of God, our being like God by living in relationship, that we walk some of the darkest valleys of despair. There are two canyons in the valley where love is distorted: *isolation* and *dependency.*

Isolation

Some of us resist life in relationship. This avoidance can take several forms: obsessive-compulsion, schizoid personality disorder, fear of intimacy, and arrogance. The classic form of this resistance is the lifestyle of the recluse or hermit. While most of us would not fall into those categories, we might share the common element in *isolation*: avoidance of life in community.

There is something in us that says, "I'd rather do it myself." Community or, to use the more literal translation of the biblical term, fellowship, is interconnected and interdependent participation in life. We are often tempted to avoid life in relationship, even when we are in a marriage, in a church, in a mission, in a business, or even in a nation's politics.

There are many experiences or tendencies that underlie this isolated approach to life. Sometimes an injury from childhood or perhaps from later life can breed a distrust of other people that leaves us bruised and nursing our wounds in isolation. Repeated injuries over multiple relationships can also breed isolation. Therapy can help with those injuries. I believe very strongly that God can use psychotherapeutic service for Christian people that is biblically based, psychologically sound, and clinically effective to help with these injuries. Ask God to guide you through a trusted referral source in the healing process and he will. (One word of caution: take as much time, effort, and ask as many questions selecting a therapist as you would buying a car! Therapists are like power or money; they can be used by God and they can also be harmful. One helpful resource is the website for the American Association of Christian Counselors at www.aacc.net.)

An isolated approach to life can also, and often does, emerge from pride. We simply think we know better than anybody else, and this can result in relationships that are abusive and resemble a form of slavery, not partnership. A person in that kind of marital relationship may not look alone; after all they're married. But the isolation in an abusive, manipulative marriage can be palpable. The controller in that kind of marriage can feel like a dictator, not a person; the spouse who is controlled can feel like property, not a person.

Pride can affect relationships other than marriage as well. It can result in political competition for tyranny, including a desire to eliminate opposition, rather than competition for democratic representation. Pride also produces businesses that are operated as monarchical kingdoms rather than a community of people working in tandem toward a common goal. Many of us have also experienced the destructive power of pride, which can erode and eventually destroy friendships.

Sometimes timidity in communication can also have isolating effects. There was a period of time during which my mother-in-law and I didn't, as we say in the south, gee-haw very well. Thankfully, that changed over time and she and I developed a cordial respect for each other. But early in our marriage my wife was hesitant to express her concerns about her mother to me; she later told me she felt isolated in her love for her mom. My conflict with her mother left my wife timid and cut off from me in fear of communication about her mother.

Those streams of isolation in the valley of relationships can be painful, whether they come from injury, pride, or timidity. God sees those experiences of isolation and he still says, "It is not good … to be alone" (Gen. 2:18).

Dependency

Dependency is the opposite of isolation. When I was a young counselor I did some study and asked some questions about dependency and its cousin, codependency. I read psychological and biblical literature and looked at experience, both mine and others'. I began to see dependency as asking an earthly relationship to do what only God can do. It is asking someone else to save us, to give us life.

One of the differences between being in love with someone and simply loving that person involves the element of dependency. In her wonderful book, *True Love Dates,* Debra Fileta discusses dependency in terms of the difference between being in love and being in need.[1] I confess to being a diehard Irish romantic, and I thoroughly enjoy the energy and beauty of a young (or old!) couple in a deeply loving relationship. But some of the energy and giddiness of being in love derives from a subconscious sense that, finally, you have found somebody who can save you. Romantic songs are full of this sentiment: here, finally, is someone who is "my everything." Sounds like God's job to me.

Many divorces occur because a spouse failed to live up to the expectations that he or she would be a good savior. When a spouse fails inevitably to be the rescuer they were contracted to be, that spouse may be exchanged for another in a series of affairs that leaves families destroyed and life unfulfilled. The dependent demand for another human being to do what only God can do is a stream that leads deeper and deeper into the valley of dysfunctional relationships.

Sometimes a dependent relationship can take the form of one spouse, usually a husband, trying to control the other person to force them to be what only God can be. One spouse can demand that the other (and sometimes children) perform the work of redemption. That kind of relationship can result in sexual, emotional, and physical abuse, "punishing" the ones who fail to give what is needed from God.

There are times when this kind of abuse occurs in the name of God's design for the husband to be the head of the household. God does, indeed, give a position of leadership to husbands and fathers (see, for example, Ephesians 5:22–33). But the leadership that comes from God is the servant leadership of someone who walks in support of the family, not a valley of harsh dictatorship, but a path of God's sacrificial love in Jesus Christ. A demand for dependency can, and often does, leave the entire family alone again. The loving leadership of Jesus Christ, on the other hand, opens the door to *climbing home* together as a family, "submitting to one another out of reverence for Christ" (Eph. 5:21, ESV).

The walk out of the valley of dependent relationships in any form includes the structure of our relationships with effective boundaries. One of the best resources for expanding the discussion of boundary formation and maintenance is the book, *Boundaries,* by Henry Cloud and John Townsend.[2] Dependency is relationship in which we fail to maintain the independence and structure of relationships with which God created us. It is important to remember in the process of relationship formation that God created humankind first as individual and only then as a person in relationship, and that means that even in a marriage we are still individuals. When I first studied boundaries years ago I mistakenly thought they were a way of advocating mutual isolation. But boundaries are not about isolation; they supply the protection and structural facilitation of relationships. They are like setting the table for a good meal. The plates, serving dishes, and eating utensils don't restrict the meal; setting the table just gives the meal structure, a place from which to eat rather than having the food splat all over the table.

THE PATHS

Jesus was, and is, brilliant. The order and internal structure of the greatest commandment and the second, like unto it, is ingenious. Jesus quoted a couple of places from the Old Testament (Deut. 6:5 and Lev. 19:18) in a combination that shows what it is like to come alive in Christ and to be what God created us to be:

> "Love the Lord your God with all your heart and with all your soul and with all your mind." This is the first and great commandment. And the second is like it: "Love your neighbor as yourself." (Matt. 22:37–39)

There is an order of significance, or dynamic order, in these verses. The foundation of life in love is God's love for us and ours for him. Our love for ourselves is next in the order. This is not a selfish, narcissistic love but the result of God's love for us: if we let God love us, his love creates healthy love for ourselves. And then we love others along with God—we love our neighbors.

The dynamic structure of life in love, or any aspect of life, is not the same as the educational structure, however. For example, walking is more significant than crawling in human function, but we need to learn to crawl before we walk; the order of significance is not the same as the order of learning. We seldom learn first to love God, then ourselves, then others. Nor do we learn right off the bat to love ourselves or others or God in a healthy way. Many of us pass through the dark valley of dysfunctional relationship formation in the process of coming to walk the path toward love in Christ. We have all, in the area of love as well as other areas, "sinned and fall[en] short of the glory of God" (Rom. 3:23).

We often come to the path leading to the love of God with our knees scraped, our hearts scarred, and our hands in need of cleansing by the grace of God. But the scars and scrapes we may bring to the path can be a gift of God's providence. The pains we experience on the way to the path upward can give us a hunger and thirst for life in God's love. Our failures in love can pave the way for the success of God's love.

The apostle Paul is an excellent example of the ways our failures shape our hunger for and capacity to receive God's love. He said,

> I am the least of the apostles and do not even deserve to be called an apostle, because I persecuted the church of God. But by the grace of God I am what I am, and his grace to me was not without effect. No, I worked harder than all of them—yet not I, but the grace of God that was with me. (1 Cor. 15:9–10)

Paul's failures in the love of God and neighbor shaped the cup into which God poured his grace and transformed Paul's life into a venue of love for all who knew him.

The cairns that lead to the heavenly places of life in the love of God are as individual as the hungers we bring and the gifts that teach us the path. Some of us learn love from parents, some from the gentle support of a grandparent, and still others from a youth director or Sunday school teacher. Our twins learned a great deal of what they know of love from each other. My sister and I learned a great deal about love from playing hide-and-seek as young children, whereas my brother and I have learned love from shared passion for music. Some of us learn the path from what has failed us in our relationships. The cairns that lead up the path toward life in love are individual because the work of God's providence and the ways his Spirit draws us to life are designed for our particular personalities, background, and environmental circumstances.

God's love for us and his bringing us into a life of love are as diverse as the ways each mother loves her children. God says through the prophet Hosea:

When Israel was a child, I loved him,
and out of Egypt I called my son....
I led them with chords of human kindness,
with ties of love.
To them I was like one who lifts
a little child to his cheek,
and I bent down to feed them. (Hosea 11:1, 4)

He does not just love humankind in general any more than a mother could love and feed her children in general. She calls and nestles and feeds them by name, one by one. God says, "I have called you by your name; you are mine" (Isa. 43:1, NKJV). Jesus "calls his own sheep by name" (John 10:3). It is he, not just any other climber, who goes before us and builds the cairns that will mark the path toward the heavenly places of his love.

There are four elements of the path of love in Christ that are common to all of us: *belovedness, family, church and community, and love for life.*

Belovedness

A person who absorbs God's love will grow toward a self-concept that he or she is loved. This *belovedness* is an essential aspect of growing up into Christ in all things (see Ephesians 4:15). Belovedness means very simply that we have a sense that we are loved, wanted, chosen to be part of the life of God. As we have seen already, belovedness means that our lives are defined in terms of God's love for us, his love through others for us, our love for ourselves, and our love for others. It means we abide in love as we abide in Christ (see John 15:1–17). The cairns that lead to this picture of ourselves as God's dearly loved children are as individual as we are, as we noted above.

For example, one of the cairns God has used to hold me in the palm of his hand, through good times and bad, is the devotional *Daily Light on the Daily Path.*[3] I had read the morning devotional for April 10 many, many times before (see Appendix D). But once, several years ago, I heard something fresh in those words. On that particular morning that devotional became, by God's Spirit, a cairn leading me up the path toward the love of God in Jesus Christ my Lord. I saw it: I am a loved delight to the God of heaven and earth! I am one of God's *beloved* children. I had finally seen the cairn.

Traditional psychologists love to talk, rightly so I believe, of self-esteem or positive self-image. Those are fine and dandy and important to a healthy life. It is not impossible to achieve those qualities by secular means, but why sit on a secular corner in front of the bank and beg when you've got an account worth millions inside? There is no self-esteem, no positive self-image greater than that which is free for the asking to anyone who will pursue their belovedness in Jesus Christ. God says,

> No longer will they call you Deserted,
> or name your land Desolate.
> …for the Lord will take delight in you,
> and your land will be married.
> …as a bridegroom rejoices over his bride,
> so will your God rejoice over you. (Isa. 62:4–5)

That describes a *family* with rich, abundant self-esteem; if you are the object of God's delight and joy, you have a life that is valued, treasured, and meaningful. That describes belovedness.

Family

The basic structure of a family is a cohesive, interconnected, and interdependent unit of parents and children. That is not a statement of morality as much as it is of biological anthropology. Whether it is a family of owls, dogs, or people, the family unit is made up of parents and children. The family rests on the marriage of one man and one woman, biblically, historically, and biologically. Unless you happen to be an amoeba, children are the fruit of one male and one female. God used this unit of husband and wife in creating humankind to be who we are and to dispel the aloneness that he found "not good" (Gen. 2:18). God, therefore, "sets the lonely in families" (Ps. 68:6). God brings his love into human relationships through this unit, and then uses the family to spread his love into the world.

There are obviously many variations on this structure. For example, adoption is one of the most beautiful and loving acts a parent can do to imitate God's adoptive grace toward the Gentiles in the New Testament. Adoption brought us one of our quite lively grandchildren. There are also many couples who may have a fine marriage, but live with the pain of infertility. Then there are many folks who live as an unmarried part of family relationships with cousins, aunts, siblings, and others. There are many others who are waiting for a relationship with a person they will be led to marry. Debra Fileta's book, *True Love Dates,* mentioned earlier in this chapter, is a very helpful, biblical, and psychologically sound guide in the process of relationship formation through dating.[4] There are also many wonderful Christian people who have little or no family of origin and are not married, but find their family in a network of friends, neighbors, mentors, and mentees who form with them a spiritual family with strong ties but no biological basis. Family structure is varied; it is not always a husband, wife, dog, cat, two children, a picket fence, and a bird in the window.

Family in any form is created by God to be a place of his love and a microcosm of the whole family, or kingdom, of God. This picture of family, both nuclear and the extended family of God, was beautifully expressed by St. Chrysostom in a prayer that reflects Jesus' statement that he is present wherever two or three are gathered in his name (see Matt. 18:20). It is also the prayer with which my wife and I ended our wedding ceremony many years ago:

> Almighty God, who hast given us grace at this time with one accord to make our common supplication unto thee, and hast promised through thy well-beloved Son that when two or three are gathered together in his Name thou wilt be in the midst of them: Fulfill now, O Lord, the desires and petitions of thy servants as may be most expedient for us; granting us in this world knowledge of thy truth, and in the world to come life everlasting. Amen.[5]

There are four elements of healthy family function we mentioned in chapter two: nurture, play, strength, and direction. These four elements help a family to come alive, grow, and enjoy life in Jesus Christ.

Nurture is feeding a family with nourishing food, emotionally, physically, and spiritually. Families are called and given the opportunity to feed one another; that responsibility becomes increasingly shared as family members grow toward adulthood. Family may consist of a group of college roommates, a nuclear family, or a neighborhood Bible study, but in all its forms family at its best is a place of nurture. I had a student several years ago who saw early on that college life and church life were difficult to coordinate. She did go to church but she also formed a Bible study group of four students—one Roman Catholic, two Church of Christ, and one Baptist! They maintained that study group throughout all four years of college and they still stay in touch for prayer, tears, and laughs. That's good family, reflecting the family of God, and it was and is a place of nurture.

Family play, also, is an essential aspect of family life and growth. We have lost the art of play in our culture because our recreation has become so dependent on resources outside of the family—movies, music, and magical electronic instruments of all kinds. The complaint that "There is nothing to do in this town" is usually more a reflection of a deficient capacity for creative play than it is a commentary on recreational resources in a community.

Across the street from our home is a park that is filled each summer with soccer for all ages. The parents come and sit in lawn chairs and enjoy watching their children learn the art of footwork, ball control, and teamwork. Now I, too, enjoy watching those kids. But the parents are right there; why not have a league where families actually play together?

When I think of family play I often think of my five sons and their families. All of them know how to do family play. They have learned from Jesus Christ that family is absolutely the best arena for recreational play in the world, and it doesn't take much money or stuff. It just takes time, love, a bit of ingenuity, and maybe a ball, some sticks for building, a tree for climbing, or shoes to run in.

Families of various kinds are also places to learn strength. Backpacking was such a gift to us during my doctoral work, though some of my professors said I would never finish my degree if I kept running off to the mountains. Backpacking was the venue for teaching our family many different kinds of strength. Our boys rode their bikes around the lake near our house nearly every day, and my wife and I worked out together and we tried to eat well. We joined together as a family to develop the strength to be comfortable with the environment and with each other at a nine- to fourteen-thousand-foot elevation. Family is a place to develop other kinds of strength as well—moral, social, vocational. God gave family as a place where love could take practical forms, feeding us with the power to live fully in Christ.

Family is a place to give and receive direction as well. I had a student who said once that his friends and family always said concerning any big decision, "We know you'll make the right choice." That kind of affirmation can give a considerable boost to self-esteem and confidence to make choices. But this student said to me that at times a lack of direction could leave him feeling somewhat adrift and lonely. And God said, "not good" (Gen. 2:18). People need the direction a family can provide for identity formation, character development, disciplined pleasure, and responsible choice-making. And by the way, that need for direction doesn't stop when a person has his or her twenty-first birthday. I consulted my parents as long as they were alive on this earth, and I consult their memory still. That honors them and helps me find direction for life.

Church

Families do not exist in a vacuum. God's Word makes it clear that just as it is "not good for the man to be alone" (Gen. 2:18), it is not good for a family to be alone. God has placed families in the c*hurch,* which is the fellowship, the community in which *family* functions in love as a microcosm of the kingdom of God.

Many Christians have a sort of love/hate relationship to the conventional church. One recent book concerning church life is Philip Yancey's largely autobiographical book, *Church: Why Bother?,* which is highly recommended as an expansion of the thoughts here.[6] That book and my own experience show that our feelings about church often emerge from formative experiences.

There are two forms of church, wonderful contexts for the family of God to learn, enjoy, and worship in his love. Church includes both a local place of worship and an extended community of God's people we attend in a variety of ways. Each is important, as Paul's letters testify. Part of his church was the place he was serving and worshiping at any one time. Another part of his church was in distant places where he had been physically present previously and would be again, but where he was for the moment present only by prayer, love, and letter.

Today Paul would attend and serve at a local assembly of God's people. He would also make use of many forms of communication, as he did in his day, to listen, teach, love, pray, and participate in an extended church well beyond his geographical location. Yes, Paul would, I believe, use the Internet, a smart phone, and he might even text. He would not be addicted to technology, though. He would, above all, do as he did in his own day and lift up Jesus Christ in whom we can come to love God, our family, our church, our neighbors, ourselves, and life itself as God's gift.

Love for Life

Children can teach us so much about love. We can distort their ability to play, learn, and love life by the layers of things and activities we pile into their lives. But a very young child can show us how to *love life.* There is a picture of one of our boys as a one-year-old, holding a piece of pine straw. That child is studying and turning and just enjoying the life out of that piece of pine straw. And of course, after I took the picture, he tried to eat it and got an "I don't like it" look on his face when he tasted the bitter pine sap. My goodness, did that child *love life.* And I have seen his children do the same things in their backyard with nothing but dirt, sticks, and a little water to make backyard "cement" so they could build a splendid fort.

The aloneness God dispelled when he created Eve was not only a door to the intimacy of marriage and love of family and church; it was a door to the love of life. Have you ever noticed that it was *after* God created Eve, *after* he created humankind as male and female, that he gave command to connect with, subdue, and to replenish the world he had made? It was a joint venture of love to which God invited Adam and

Eve, and to which he invites us anew in our life in Jesus Christ. We are called a "new creation" in Jesus Christ (2 Cor. 5:17). The sin of Adam and Eve, our sin, is connecting with life, with the creation, outside of our fellowship with God. Sin entered when humankind sought to rise to equality with God, "knowing good and evil" (Gen. 3:5). Sin is trying to love life apart from God; righteousness is loving life with God through Jesus Christ.

THE HEAVENLY PLACES

The biblical word *joy* captures the meaning of *love for life.* Two books of the New Testament are saturated with the word *joy:* Philippians and 1 John. Ironically both books were written in a time of spiritual and physical stress to the Christian faith. Philippians was written during one of Paul's Roman imprisonments (see Philippians 1:12–26). And yet some form of the word "joy" is used multiple times in the book. Paul says, "Rejoice in the Lord always. I will say it again: Rejoice!" (Phil. 4:4).

And 1 John was written during a time of spiritual stress through dissension in the Christian community (see for example 1 John 2:18, 19; 4:1–5), but reminds the readers that "Whoever has the Son has life" (1 John 5:12). And when that life is filled with the love of God it brings a love of life and is characterized by joy.

Several years ago I was asked to preach a baccalaureate service for a graduating high school class. I preached from Philippians 4:1–4. Now sometimes the joy of the Lord is seen as a serious, somewhat religious thing. I studied that passage and the context of the joy of the Lord in the new creation we become in Jesus Christ. That led me back to Adam and Eve before the fall. I made the connection between the new creation, the untrammeled and pure pleasure of God's children before the fall, and the joy of the Lord. And I smiled. I said to those seniors, "If you can find anything, anything that will give you more enjoyment of life, more love for life than following Jesus Christ, then go there if that is your choice. But I am here to tell you, graduates, to tell you from the Word of God and from my own experience, you will never find anything that will teach you to love life, live to the full, and experience the joy with which God put us on this earth more than by following Jesus Christ. Jesus Christ is the door to the enjoyment of life."

That joy is the heavenly place of life in God's love.

THE QUESTIONS AND SCRIPTURES

1. Do you have a sense that you are loved? Why or why not? If Jesus took a walk with you for thirty minutes, how would that affect your sense that you are loved, your experience of belovedness? Could you take that walk in his presence this week?
2. Do you ever find yourself pushing against those nearest to you? Or do you ever feel dependent on or controlled by those closest to you? Do you ever feel both isolated and craving for dependence?
3. Who in your life has most represented God's love to you? To whom have you been a significant instrument of God's love?
4. What does your church look like? (Friends? Family? Bible study? People you sit in church pews with?) Are most of them in your local church?
5. How would God want to love you this next week? If you let him love you in that way, what effect would that have on your loved ones? On your love for yourself?
6. How would God want you to love yourself this week? If you love yourself that way, what effect would that have on your loved ones? On your love for God?
7. How would God want to love through you this week? What do you need to do for that to happen? (For example begin to deal with your fear of intimacy, forgive someone, forgive yourself, etc.)
8. Scripture for further reflection: Song of Sol. 1–8; Hosea 11:1–11; John 13:1–17, 15:1–17, 17:6–24; 1 Cor. 13; 1 John 4:7–21.

CHAPTER 7

CHOICES: WHO COMES FIRST?

Our twins asked us a question the moment they were born. On Dec. 15, 1980 they came into the world struggling to live, finally giving their parents unbelievable relief by screaming out for the breath of life, and eventually squirming around in the incubators that gave support to their premature lives. They were eight weeks early. And they demanded, along with their brother who was eighteen months older, the answer to a question. It was a question each parent of multiple children has asked at one time or another.

"Who will be first? Whom will you love most? How will you divide up your love for us?" Sometimes it was a rather funny question. Every parent knows the experience of each child wanting to get dessert or a toy or a horseback ride first. "Me first, Daddy, me first!" Sound familiar? We wrestled with that question for months, attempting what every parent tends to want to do, to love each of them equally. But long before we ever taught them anything, our children taught us: equality of love just wasn't the answer.

We began to ask about our heavenly Father's love. Does he have favorites? Does he divide his love equally? It took hours, months of thought and prayer. Calder and I had many talks about the dynamics of our love for these three wonderful boys. The answer came to me one morning during devotions and journaling: God loves each of us with all he has to give, with the gift of his Son. Jesus is "the firstborn among many brothers and sisters" (Rom. 8:29), and because we are clothed in his life, we have the position of the firstborn along with him. We are co-heirs with Jesus Christ (see Romans 8:17 and Ephesians 3:6). Paul prays that we "may be filled with all the fullness of God" (Eph. 3:19, ESV). Each of us gets God's fullness.

That was the answer: we would love each of our children the most! Each of them would be first. God had created the parenting pattern by giving all he had for us. His example said, "Don't divide up what you give. Give first place to each as God gave first place to each person for whom Christ died." There were times when we put this insight into practice through what we called "special times." These times would belong only to one of the boys, singled out as "first for the day," to go on a hike, get a milkshake, or just go to the store. On another day, someone else would get a "special time." Each son was first.

The good news of Jesus Christ proclaims that God loved us before he ever spoke the Word that flung the stars across the sky. John beautifully describes the initiative of God's love for us; he chose us before we chose him:

> In the beginning was the Word, and the Word was with God, and the Word was God. He was with God in the beginning. Through him all things were made; without him nothing was made that has been made.…
>
> To all who did receive him, to those who believed in his name, he gave the right to become children of God—children born not of natural descent, nor of human decision or a husband's will, but born of God. (John 1:1–3, 12–13)

Paul says that God "chose us in him before the creation of the world" (Eph. 1:4). If we ever come to put Christ first in our lives, God is already way ahead of us. He said he called Jeremiah (see Jeremiah 1:5), his servant Israel (see Isaiah 49:1), and the apostle Paul (see Galatians 1:15) from within their mothers' wombs to become agents of his love in the world.

We may think, even as Christian people, that the most important first choice in our lives is our choice to accept Christ, to follow him, to grow in him, to love and live in him. But that is not first in our lives. Before we ever accept Christ, before we ever do any of our sin or righteousness or love or hope or faith, before we ever draw breath or wake in the morning, God chooses us. He chooses to love us, to sustain us, and to give us yet another day. The first light of day is the sign of God's choice that precedes all our choice-making, working, failing, loving, losing, winning, and all our living.

Jeremiah was dismayed at the sin of God's people, their rejection of the message God had sent through him, and the seeming futility of serving God. He became despondent, depressed, and struggled toward the choice to continue as God's prophet. He said,

> I remember my affliction and my wandering,
> the bitterness and the gall.
> I well remember them,
> and my soul is downcast within me.
> Yet this I call to mind
> and therefore I have hope:
> Because of the Lord's great love
> we are not consumed,
> for his compassions never fail.
> They are new every morning;
> great is your faithfulness. (Lam. 3:19–23)

The choice that sustained Jeremiah was not the choice of the people of God or even his own choice; it was the choice of God not to abandon his people, to remain faithful to them, in spite of their choices to abandon him.

Job complained that God had unjustly abandoned him in his suffering. He saw his choices as first in his life, his choices to conduct his life as "blameless and upright, a man who fears God and shuns evil" (Job 1:8). But Job learned that long before he chose to live in a godly way, God chose for him to live, and for his world to be inhabited with horses and light and crocodiles and waves and mountains and earth and sky. God asked Job, "Have you ever given orders to the morning, or shown the dawn its place, that it may take the earth by its edges?" (Job 38:12–13).

When Job repented, he did not repent of sin; he repented of thinking that any of his choosing or living or blameless conduct was first. He learned, after he had not only heard about God but had seen him, that he had only lived and made choices and enjoyed his life because God woke the day each morning with a word that said, "Live yet another day, Job."

Jesus said, "You did not choose me, but I chose you and appointed you so that you might go and bear fruit…" (John 15:16). Paul said, "We are his workmanship, created in Christ Jesus for good works, which God prepared beforehand that we should walk in them" (Eph. 2:10). And the writer of 1 John puts the whole "Who is first?" issue in one simple verse: "We love because he first loved us" (1 John 4:19). God's love precedes all our loves; God's faithfulness precedes all our faith; God's choosing us precedes all our choices for him. Our choices, at their best, rest on his choices.

This is good news because when our faith fails us—and it will—God remains faithful to us. Every Christian counselor who reads these words has seen clients or patients who fear that God has abandoned them because of some sin or weakness. A child's confidence in being loved can wobble if that love depends on athletic or academic achievement, beauty, compliance, or any other good choices. What if he or she loses a race, makes a bad grade, or gets pimples? Will the love diminish or disappear? Christians who believe their faith in God is more important than God's faithfulness to them can, likewise, feel spiritually unstable and vulnerable if their faith in God wavers. Will God decide he doesn't want to mess with us anymore? Very simply, we believe because God first came to us; we follow Christ because he first seeks us when we are lost; "we love because he first loved us" (1 John 4:19).

THE VALLEYS

The message of the Bible is that God in Jesus Christ is not first because we make him first; he can *become* first in our lives only because he *is* first. "He is before all things, and in him all things hold together" (Col. 1:17). Jesus is, according to Hebrews 12:2 "the founder…of our faith…" (ESV), "the author…of our faith" (NKJV), and "the pioneer…of our faith" (NIV). Regardless of the translation, Jesus is first. If we put our choices first, we are making an idol of ourselves and are vulnerable to worshiping our faith rather than God. We enter and languish in the valley of despair if our choice takes priority over God's choice to pour his grace into us. Paul cried out concerning the futility of putting our obedience first, "O wretched man that I am!" (Rom. 7:24). The tendency to idolize our faith is seen in the *Pharisees* in Jesus' day and in *pietism* in more recent church history.

The Pharisees

The *Pharisees* were not idolatrous because they loved Scripture; they became idolatrous because they used Scripture to make themselves and their traditions first rather than God. Their giving priority to their faith made it impossible for them to hear God; they were so wedded to their understanding of God's Word that God could not say anything to them. Have you ever had a conversation in which you were so sure about what the other person was going to say that you couldn't hear what he or she actually did say? That is pharisaical listening: listening with your mind made up what you're going to hear. The Pharisee in each of us believes that we already hear and see all that we need to know of God and life and the world; it is others who are blind and deaf. But Jesus said, referring to one of his conflicts with the Pharisees, "For judgment I have come into this world, so that the blind will see and those who see will become blind" (John 9:39).

Pietism

Pietism has the same effect of obscuring the work of God by its focus on our work for God. Piety in itself is a good thing, of course. It has to do with devotion and reverence for God. But pietism can become focused on the devotion and reverence rather than the God who was revered and the object of devotion. It's a question, again, of what comes first. If the focus is on which pew I sit in or what hymns we sing or the stained glass in the window rather than the Lord of the church, God can be obscured by our worship. The goal is "that in all things he may have the preeminence" (Col. 1:18).

Jesus illustrates the valley of putting our faith first in the parable of the Pharisee and the tax collector. The Pharisee was quite impressed with his faith and obedience to God, and he was quick to let God know he put

God first in everything. The tax collector, on the other hand, prayed in humility that God would be merciful to him in his sinfulness. Jesus said of the tax collector: "I tell you that this man…went home justified before God. For all who exalt themselves will be humbled, and those who humble themselves will be exalted" (Luke 18:14). The Pharisee put his faith first; the tax collector prayed for God to first be merciful to him.

The valley of *pietism* and *pharisaism,* or putting faith first and God second, can be illustrated by a husband or wife who is so focused on how wonderful their love is that they forget their anniversary, their spouse's birthday, or the fact that their spouse has a cold. It would be like a husband being so insistent on giving his wife a wonderful meal at an expensive restaurant that he ignores the fact that his wife has a terrible cold, can't taste the food, and would rather be curled up under the covers at home with some hot tea! That wife would much prefer her husband focus a little less on how wonderful his love is and a little more on how wonderful she is!

THE PATHS

If we rest on God's choice to be who he is in the gift of Jesus Christ, we can choose to be who we are as God's children. If we let our choices rest on God's choice to love us, live in us, grow us into his image, and use us in his service, our lives will be increasingly filled with the fruit of the Spirit (Gal. 5:22–23) and the fruit of God's work through us (John 15:1–17).

There are at least three cairns on the path to our choosing Christ first on the foundation of his choosing us first: *small steps, inclusiveness,* and *focus on Christ.* Very simply, when we follow Christ above everything else in our lives, our choices in *small steps* of obedience will lead to more positive choices, they will grow toward *inclusive* love for all of life and all those God loves, and also toward exclusive *focus on Christ.*

Small Steps

One small, good choice tends to produce more good choices. One of the major contributions of the Mental Research Institute, a founding body of marriage and family therapy, was the development of theory and techniques for change through small steps.[1] The work of those psychotherapeutic pioneers can be applied to our spiritual choices and health as well. Obedience to God in the area of devotional life, for example, will tend to produce obedience to God in parenting, in giving, and in sensitivity to one's spouse. Any choice we make to put Christ first in our lives will show us the need to put him first in other areas.

There is a residual effect of both good and evil in our lives. Tell one lie, and a person must keep fabricating more lies to be consistent with the first lie. Do something good for someone, and the reinforcing feelings that accompany that initial good tends to produce more good. A small argument with a spouse can escalate to a major battle; a small act of love can escalate to a wonderful time of shared marital love and pleasure. It is amazing in counseling how powerful one small, healthy act can be in changing the dynamics of a person's life. Or, to use a common illustration, you can throw a small stone in a pond at any number of places to create ripples that will reach the shore.

Jesus used this principle in his teaching. He would often call people to choose to follow him by emphasis on an area he knew would be effectively appealing. He knew the blind would like to see, the lame to walk, and a fisherman would like to catch some fish. He used those areas to stimulate a choice to follow him, knowing that an expanded discipleship would follow. But we sometimes want to solve the hard problems and accomplish major acts of obedience first. Our choice to follow Christ sometimes focuses on a more difficult area than on an area that would be more productive.

For example, I have at times in my life had trouble with peanut butter. It's almost like I've switched addictions: peanut butter on crackers, on hot, toasted homemade bread, on an apple, or peanut butter right off the spoon. Now peanut butter in moderation can be a gift (and what a gift!) of God. But when I realized I was eating way too much peanut butter, I feared I had become powerless over peanut butter and that my consumption thereof had become unmanageable. So I tried one of the things I've used with clients who have difficulty with excess in any area. I decided I would not eat a single bite of peanut butter for which I could not thank God. It seemed a simple self-assignment, but guess what: after a moderate few bites, I found I couldn't thank God for the seventh or even the fifth bite of peanut butter. One tablespoon, twice a week on Calder's toasted homemade bread—now that I could thank God for. The choice to thank God before every bite of peanut butter led eventually to moderation. The *small step* of giving thanks had a residual effect on my peanut butter habits.

Growth Toward Inclusiveness

None of us loves everybody God loves. But we can grow toward a willingness to *include* everyone as potential recipients of our love. We tend to practice a kind of cultural, political, social, or moral election of those to whom we will choose to show God's saving work. Sometimes our exclusion of certain people is kind of funny, other times more tragic. The question of willingness to love precedes the action and attitude of love. Are we willing, for example, to show the same love to all who attend our church? Are we willing to show God's love to all who live in the neighborhood of our church? Are we willing to show that love and affirmation to a follower of Christ whose denomination or theology or lifestyle is different from ours?

It doesn't matter whether the shape of your theology affirms Christ's saving work only for the elect or you believe Christ died for all, God calls us to bring the gospel to the whole world. Jesus said, "Go and make disciples of all nations…" (Matt. 28:18). We will see in the next chapter that not all of us are called to do everything, but a part of healthy life in Christ includes a choice to follow Jesus in his love for all, and not to refuse God's good news to any because we don't like them for one reason or another. If we choose to put Christ first in our lives, we will grow toward increasingly including all we meet as the recipients of God's gifts through us.

We will also grow toward inclusive love and respect for other Christians. God's people are found in some unexpected places and groups, and they don't always look like we think they should. When I went to Alcoholics Anonymous back in the late 70s, God opened my heart to include some folks that I didn't always agree with on everything. Many Alcoholics Anonymous members talked rough, looked rough, and had lived rough. And my initial response was to give them the looks I received years later for my white shirt and tie. Surely these folks weren't real Christians. But then a strange thing happened; God began to teach me through these rough-talking, rough-looking folks. My choice to become sober led to putting Christ first because he had put me first. And when I put Christ first, that led to my inclusive respect for these ministers of Alcoholics Anonymous.

The principle of growth toward inclusiveness is founded on the extension of God's love to the whole world: He "so loved the world that he gave his one and only Son…" (John 3:16). God then expanded that love when he included the Gentiles in the church. It is very difficult for us to understand how hard it was for Jewish Christians to offer the gospel to the Gentiles and then to include the Gentiles in the church's fellowship (see for example Acts 11:4–18 and Galatians 2:11–16). Those early Christians were able to grow toward inclusiveness as an imitation of the inclusiveness of God's love.

Focus on Christ

Many Christians today in what has been called the evangelical movement recognize that "Jesus Christ is Lord" (Phil. 2:11) and that he is preeminent in all things, over any preacher, denomination, theological system, or political orientation. The churches at Corinth seemed to have difficulty with this exclusive focus on Jesus Christ. They were rather divided between those who followed Apollos, Peter, Paul, and those who claimed to follow Christ alone (see 1 Corinthians 1:10–3:23).

The choice to put Christ first, with the foundation of that choice being that he loved us first, is a theme of the theology of Karl Barth. This Swiss theologian exploded the liberal theological world in 1918 with his commentary on Paul's Epistle to the Romans.[2] Barth spent his life developing, refining, and applying his Christ-centered theology to the pastoral, political, and ecclesiastical world of the European and eventually the worldwide church.

Toward the end of his life, Barth stated this theme simply and beautifully in a radio interview. He said,

> The last word that I have to say as a theologian or politician is

> not a concept like grace but a name: Jesus Christ. He is grace and he is the ultimate one beyond world and church and even theology.... And my own concern in my long life has been increasingly to emphasize this name and to say: "In him." In him is grace. In him is the spur to work, warfare, and fellowship. In him is all that I have attempted in my life in weakness and folly. It is there in him.[3]

There is a story that seems to be based on a factual account of a question-and-answer session after one of Barth's lectures when he toured the United States in 1962. The story is that a student asked if Barth could summarize his theology in one sentence. He said, according to the story that is now part of preachers' legend, "Yes I can, in the words of a song I learned at my mother's knee: 'Jesus loves me, this I know, for the Bible tells me so.'"

THE HEAVENLY PLACES

God had a picture. He knew what he wanted when he first raised the sun in the sky and then placed humankind on the earth. He wanted companionship, the sharing of his glory, and life in prodigal joy. What a gift! The world was humankind's birthday present. The world of that first sunrise and the raising of Adam and Eve out of the earth was "...very good" (Gen. 1:31).

Sin ruined the painting of God, which had been so good. But the good news of Jesus Christ is that God has restored the painting; he has renewed the good life he made. God started all over, painting his new creation with a brush filled with blood and irradiated by the first light of Easter, drawing into the fabric of his work a multitude called the Church, all those who follow Christ into this art of the love of God.

God has a picture still. He knows what he wants each day when he raises the sun in your sky and then plants your feet for one more day on the earth. He wants companionship, the sharing of his glory, and life in prodigal joy. What a gift! The world is his gift to you—every day. In a way, God places you daily in the dawn of a new creation.

What does it look like for us to put Christ first, to recognize his centrality in the painting of God's new creation? It looks like:

> [T]he light of the morning when the sun rises, a morning without clouds, like the tender grass springing out of the earth, by clear shining after rain. (2 Sam. 23:4, NKJV)

> God's love…poured out into our hearts through the Holy Spirit. (Rom. 5:5)

> [T]he peace…which transcends all understanding. (Phil. 4:7)

> [W]hatever is true, whatever is noble, whatever is right, whatever is pure, whatever is lovely, whatever is admirable…excellent or praiseworthy. (Phil. 4:8)

> …birth through the word of truth, that we might be a kind of firstfruits of all [God] created. (James 1:18)

It looks like the rising of Jesus Christ from our death in his body. It looks like Jesus Christ, raised to new life in us, living in us, working in us, playing and running and spending and saving and giving in us. It looks like God loving in us, Christ living in us, the Spirit working in us. That is what it looks like for us to put Christ first because he put saving us first. It looks like Jesus Christ, walking this earth and loving all life, in you, in me, in the Church, in his new creation.

THE QUESTIONS AND SCRIPTURES

1. Do you have more faith in your faith or in God's faithfulness? Try journaling for a week or a month about God's work in your life. Then go back and reread what you wrote. How many lines speak about God's work and how many lines talk about your work?
2. What might you gain if each new day began with your thoughts and feelings fixed on Christ? (And what would you lose if you did that?) What if in that way you "let the

message of Christ dwell in you richly" (Col. 3:16)?

3. If God's love for you became the foundation of your life, what three things would you do differently (for example, I would talk to my spouse more often, spend more time with my children, pray each night as I fall asleep, change a business practice, etc.)?
4. If you were God's favorite person on earth, what need would he meet in you? Has he already provided for what you need?
5. If you gave your family as much priority as God has given you, what would you do differently with spouse and children?
6. What bothered you most in this chapter? Was it a concern regarding writing style? Theology? Was it something that needs to change in your priorities?
7. What one small step will you take to draw closer to God and to your loved ones this week? What will you do during the rest of this day to move in that direction?
8. Scripture for further reflection: Deut. 30:11–20; Josh. 24:14–27; Mark 10:35–45; John 6:26–51; Acts 11:4–18; Rom. 9:6–29; Eph. 2:1–10; Col. 1:15–20, 2:6–12.

CHAPTER 8

VALUE: WHAT IS WORTHWHILE?

Tara, our adopted German Shepherd mix dog, has a covenant with God (see Genesis 9:12). She shows it, too. Sometimes I learn things from her that I haven't learned in all my years of education, ministry, and listening to the wisdom of those I have served. She walked with us several years ago to the top of Brown's Pass in central Colorado, and sat looking intently, almost worshipfully, at the vista of the Continental Divide spreading out before us. She has shown the same gaze, the same appreciation and scrutiny of the landscape, looking at the park across from our house. She valued the same things in each place. The two places are quite different, one dramatically beautiful and one sort of ordinary. Each place gave her an opportunity to do something she valued: She could be with the people she loved.

There are other things Tara values, of course: food, play, sleep, and other basic needs common to all dogs, but when that girl looks at us with those big, brown eyes and says by her intense stare that she loves being with us, she leaves no doubt as to her highest values. She values relationship with her folks. Occasionally, I read a devotional passage out loud to my wife and Tara inevitably nestles into a soft place, groans with pleasure, and blinks her eyes as if she understands every word. She doesn't, but she does understand the special togetherness we all have when I read those devotionals. She hears the tone, the cadence of the words, the sense that there is an unseen presence there—and she loves being together with us.

That was a lesson I learned from the dissertation I wrote several years ago titled, *Values, Therapeutic Alliance, and Marital Therapy: A Study of the Therapist-Client Relationship in Marital Therapy.*[1] The study has, in fact, shaped my work in ministry, teaching, and counseling for many years. It concludes, in part, that it is more important to value a person than to value one's own values. Specifically, this would mean that it is more important to value a person's needs as a human being than whether or not that person agreed with my political, denominational, or other values.

That is precisely what Jesus did when he gave his life on the Cross for the whole world of people he came to save, not just conservatives, liberals, Americans, Germans, Methodists, Presbyterians, or Catholics. Jesus valued the people he came to love into life through his death, resurrection, present life, and his coming again. He valued those whom he came to save more than he valued the approval of the Pharisees or Sadducees.

That is the way Tara loves being with us. We have seen her have a choice between a walk with us and eating her breakfast; she'll grab a bite then bound toward the door, tail wagging, eyes bright, and ready for the leash. We have seen her enjoying a wonderful nap, softly snoring with an occasional deep sigh, and then if she hears us go out the back door or gather her leash from the wall, she's wide awake and ready to be with us. My dissertation was a fine thing. But I could have learned some of the same things, though perhaps not as scientifically, by observing Jesus or watching my dog.

Values represent the belief in good and the action and feelings associated with that belief. Values are faith and love in action. Values are the practical, behavioral form of loving God, ourselves, each other, and life, because God first loved us. One of the New Testament books that deals clearly with values is Philippians; Paul prays that the Philippian Christians will "approve the things that are excellent" (Phil. 1:11, NKJV). And he concludes his letter directing Christians to meditate on what is "true… noble…right…pure…lovely…admirable" (Phil. 4:8). If we believe it is good when they say to us, "Let us go to the house of the Lord," we'll get dressed and go to church. If we believe it is a good thing to hear God speak, we'll open the Bible, read a book, listen to a sermon, or take the sacrament and attend to what we hear. If we believe that praise music is a fine thing, we'll sing and raise our hands in praise. If we believe the sometimes soft and at other times strong strains of a Bach cantata contribute to our relationship with God, then we will listen to that kind of music.

What exactly is worthwhile? We need our lives to be significant. Our lives cannot be significant if our energy is spent on insignificant trivia. Jesus said, "Where your treasure is, there your heart will be also" (Matt. 6:21). Ironically, sometimes our four-legged sons and daughters like Tara know that better than we, for we so easily get trapped in the valley of treasuring the insignificant.

THE VALLEYS

Two dynamic elements prevent our ascending the path to values fulfillment: *acquisition* and *aggression*. The first of these elements emerges from an underlying belief that the more we have of desirable stuff, the better our life will be. We're sort of like the child in the movie series *Home Alone* who seemed to believe that if ice cream is good, then the more ice cream we have, the better life is. But then if we have a lot of good stuff—a good spouse, house, church, car, business, or nation—we can be sure that other folks will be trying to get our things. Therefore, the dark valley of destructive values becomes walled by *aggression* to defend our valued life.

Acquisition

Jesus knew that we tend to believe if a barn is good, then a bigger barn must be better (see Luke 12:13–21). There is a drive in our values to get more and more of what seems to bring us satisfaction. Years ago a man and I sat near a campfire in the rain in the Cruces Basin Wilderness in northern New Mexico. He was one of the leaders on a backpacking trip sponsored by the Northwest Texas Conference of the United Methodist Church. This man was quite athletic, had a wonderful family, was a very effective leader in his church, and gave a great deal to support church programs financially. We talked of bears, backpacking equipment, and exercise programs to prepare for outdoor activity. Then he said, "Madoc, I need to ask you something; have you ever known anyone that had money, I mean real money, lots of it?" I said yes, I'd known one or two, thinking of some folks in one of my churches. He then asked, quietly and with deep feeling, "Did you ever know any of those people who had money and felt it was enough?"

I asked, "Do you find contentment to be a struggle?" We talked of the need for God to heal the drive of *acquisition,* the compulsion to get more and more and more of the good stuff of life while never coming to a point of real joy, gratitude, and gladness for whatever our lot may happen to be. Through that conversation and our continued contact afterward, that man began to develop a set of values that brought him out of the valley of constant compulsion toward more and more acquisition to a point of simplicity, gratitude, and relaxed but productive life. His family saw him more, his girls came to know him as a loving father, and his church knew him as a still-generous but much less controlling giver. His values had progressed out of the valley of the shadow of the death of acquisition and toward a life valuing above all the relationships with family, church, God, and himself. He was content.

Aggressiveness

That man's employees and competitors especially saw the change God had brought to his values. Prior to that campfire discussion and many others talks that followed, he was a mean competitor and retentively stingy with his employees. He *aggressively* held on to all he had and defended his property in such a way that he kept people, even family, friends, and employees, at arm's length. He was rich in stuff. He was relationally impoverished.

Most of what psychologists call defensiveness is essentially protecting what we feel we must have in order to live. We protect our egos, families, political positions, churches, righteousness, wealth, castles, and lives because we fear that somebody else is surely lurking and about to pounce on the treasures that make our lives worthwhile. That defensive aggressiveness is especially destructive in marital, family, and other close relationships. Many counselors have seen marriages torn apart by an aggressive desire to win, to be right and prove the other wrong.

The culture in which we live does not exactly make it easy to escape the valley of *acquisition* and *aggressive* defense of what we've acquired, however. We get paid for being energetically, even compulsively, driven to get more and more of whatever we value—more money, education, sex, play, victories, bigger churches, better-selling books, bigger houses, more cars, guns, Bibles, and positions of authority. But the more we get, the emptier we feel. We wind up in tears sitting by a campfire asking about the painfulness of our lives. We cry out for a path forward, to a heavenly place of value where our lives can be both productive and focused on the things that matter.

A disclaimer is important at this point. There is a legitimate place for both productive acquisition and aggressive defense of what we love. There's nothing wrong with making a living or defending our country. It is only when we attribute more value to what we have than who we're with that our values become a skewed source of pain and frustration. Tara loves the park across from our house and the trails of Colorado and New Mexico, but if she left the people she loves in order to live in the park or on the trails, she'd be an unhappy pup; she would have left the path toward the heavenly places, the path of focus on relationship.

THE PATHS

Two cairns mark the path toward the heavenly places of Christ-centered values: *satisfaction* and *connection*. I don't believe either one of these is easy to follow. For example, dieticians have studied for years to discover the exact combination of foods that bring lasting nutritional *satisfaction*. Some of the most satisfying behaviors of our lives are quite counterintuitive, like the discipline necessary to achieve a high degree of athletic, artistic, or professional expertise. Furthermore, we often can think we have more *connection* with things of value than we really do. So this path is a challenging one.

Satisfaction

This concerns the values that are really worthwhile, which really leave us happy, filled, and glad. Do you remember eating some meals that left you uncomfortably stuffed and others that left you uncomfortably hungry? The question of satisfaction concerns finding the life meal that is "just right," and that leaves us pleasantly nourished. There are at least four stones that can contribute to the cairn of satisfaction in our values:

others' input, history, balance, and *timing.*

Other people can sometimes see our own happiness or unhappiness better than we. Their observations can help us find the values that can bring us satisfaction. There was a time that I thought I wanted above all to be a great preacher. Counseling was fine for some folks, but I'd rather be preaching, preferably in a big church. But my wife knew me. She made the observation one time that I seemed to get the greatest satisfaction from working with individuals, couples, or families in counseling, hospital visits, funerals, premarital work, and home visits. She even suggested that the time might come that I might go back to school to study counseling. I replied, "I would never leave the ministry." I didn't leave the ministry, but God sure did reshape my ministry to focus on one person at a time. Calder helped me learn what would be more deeply satisfying for me than just preaching.

Sometimes a study of history, both our own story and others', can contribute a stone to the cairn on the path toward values satisfaction. When you study your life or the lives of others, what values seem to be the most satisfying? Who are the people whose values seem to you to bring the most joy? Do the people with the biggest barns and bank accounts have the most *satisfaction*? What about those with the most letters after their names?

A study of history led one of our sons to pursue ministry in the Presbyterian Church in America. I asked him years ago what led him in that direction, thinking it may have been a deficiency he saw in the theology of his United Methodist father! It turns out that it didn't have anything to do with that, but rather a Christmas gift my wife and I gave him. We had found a biography of Stonewall Jackson on sale and, knowing our son's love for history and civil war history especially, gave him that book for Christmas.[2] It was a quite thick book but he devoured every word. He saw how Jackson's faith in the sovereign care of God could bring a satisfying peace in a changing and sometimes dangerous world. That image led in part to our son adopting the Reformed tradition of the Christian faith. That study contributed a major stone in the cairn leading to our son's ministerial satisfaction.

Another essential stone in the cairn on the values path is balance. Many years ago Karl Menninger's picture of mental health was published under the title *The Vital Balance*.[3] An often-quoted verse says, "A false balance is an abomination to the Lord" (Prov.11:1, ESV). That specific reference concerns the balances used in measuring business transactions, but applies to all of life. This is especially important in assessing the role of values in relation to activities, possessions, or behaviors that are good, but are not God. Money, houses, denomination, food, education, sleep, and all the other pleasant things of our lives can enhance our enjoyment of life in Christ. It is when we live for these good things as if they are as important as our relationships with each other, ourselves, and God that they become destructive.

The need for balance in order for values to function properly is apparent in athletic training. If all training is focused on one muscle group, the body can become unbalanced. If all training is focused on diet with no exercise, the body may be well nourished but still fail to function properly athletically. One of the most common and debilitating injuries in backpacking and climbing is an ankle sprain. Years ago, when we were backpacking a good deal, our training was not complete until we spent time doing ankle exercises by walking on uneven ground covered with loose, softball- to basketball-sized rock. Our cairn of athletic training needed to be balanced.

Perhaps the most challenging stone of the cairn on the values path to satisfaction is timing, or delay. When I read the section on delayed gratification in Scott Peck's book *The Road Less Traveled* years ago, I became so irritated I put the book down and didn't finish it until years later.[4] Delayed gratification is particularly repugnant in our society. We want the things we value right now, thank you very much. Perhaps two of the best teachers of the significance of delayed gratification in the path to satisfaction are eating and marital sexual activity. Each of those ways of enjoying life in Christ is best done slowly, with prolonged gratitude. God uses the bodies he's given us to bring deeply satisfying blessing only if we're not in too big a hurry!

Connection

Both eating and marital sexual activity also illustrate the importance of *connection* on the path to experiencing the values of life in Christ. We live in a drive-thru society with drive-through attitudes. One of the biggest differences between classical and pop literature, music, and art is the time it takes to connect. Pop culture, including Christian pop culture, is fast; it moves fast; even if it is slow it lasts only a few minutes! A symphony or a gourmet meal, on the other hand, take a great deal more time and so allow us to connect more deeply. There are newscasters on TV that my wife and I enjoy. Now we are quite aware of the fact that we grew up in the southeastern part of America and talk real slow, but my goodness, we have to turn on closed captioning to understand what the mile-a-minute news folks are saying! Could you hear one of those newscasters reading a psalm or a Robert Frost poem at that fast rate? Imagine it!

Our experience of the path toward the heavenly places of values in Christ means we slow down, take a breath, and connect with the experiences God uses to love us into the fullness of his presence.

THE HEAVENLY PLACES

There was a time when I thought the painting "American Gothic" by Grant Wood was a good picture of the heavenly places of good values.[5] Do you recall it? The painting shows a farmer and his spinster daughter standing with a stoic, not-at-all-happy look on their faces. I always thought a good title of the painting would be "Life is hard and don't you dare smile about it!" Jesus has shown quite a different picture.

The heavenly places of values focused in Christ are really an endpoint of *Climbing Home* as a whole. This life in these heavenly places, these mountains of hope, are a precursor to life in the pleasures at God's right hand (see Psalm 16:11). Two elements occupy this particular meadow of life in God's presence: *contentment* and *loyalty*.

Contentment

My father was not a perfect man but he did teach his children and friends the joy of *contentment.* Once toward the end of his life we asked if he wouldn't like to have a bigger TV; his eyesight was fading and some of us thought a bigger screen would be nice. He was appreciative and gracious as he usually was when offered a gift or favor, but he said, "I don't really need a bigger TV as long as I can tell the difference between a replay and the real thing. What I'd really like is probably something you couldn't give me; I'd like for the Atlanta Braves' hitting to be as good as their pitching! If you could deliver that to my TV screen, that'd be just splendid." He was content with what he had, as long as the Braves could deliver a win now and then.

The contentment of Christian values comes into focus in 1 Timothy 6. That passage shows, on the one hand, the frustration and dissatisfaction that can come from placing value on transitory stuff like money or the size of a TV screen. The writer says those kinds of values lead to a loss of faith and "many sorrows" (1 Tim. 6:10, NKJV). That same chapter advocates focusing our values and trust for security on "God, who richly provides us with everything for our enjoyment" (1 Tim. 6:17). The apostle Paul reflected this same sense of contentment when he wrote, from prison no less, that in Christ he had learned to be content both with little or much (see Philippians 4:11–12).

The belief that underlies contentment in Christ is a conviction that we are a wealthy, blessed, joyful people as God's children. We're alive in Christ, not dead as doornails! There is an invitation within the principle of contentment in the heavenly places in Christ that is often neglected. It is the permission, invitation even, to allow ourselves to be anointed by the goodness of God in the gifts he chooses for each of us. The will of God is a far cry from the stalwart and stolid "American Gothic." His will for us is that we have life and have it abundantly (see John 10:10).

That does not mean that each person, each nation, or each family will be blessed with the same prosperity and joy. God enriches all of our lives with his blessings; God does not enrich all of our lives with the same blessings. One person may have little or no money or prestige but be an outstanding soccer player, gifted by God with the ability to keep a ball in the air for long periods followed by a swift kick into the corner of a net. Another person may have little or no athletic ability but be blessed with a rich and wonderful family—siblings, grandparents, dogs, cats, and kids gamboling around like joyful deer in the yard. It is part of the heavenly places of values centered in Christ that we discover, enjoy, cultivate, and share the particular blessings that are uniquely ours.

Loyalty

That kind of contentment leads to *loyalty.* We live in a society in which the grass is perpetually greener on the other side of the fence. It doesn't help that the advertising world has become extremely skilled at feeding the sense that our lives will be good only if we change our house, our insurance company, our town, our playground, or our clothes. Sometimes the goal seems to be that our lives return to another developmental stage when we were really glad and happy about our lives as they were. We are told that if we take this pill, join this spa, use this makeup, or eat this diet then we'll have the sexual, financial, and physical prowess of our earlier lives.

How many books, ads, or even sermons invite us to the joys of our lives just as they are?

There was a period of time during which it was common for United Methodist preachers to change churches quite often. The first churches to which I was appointed had hardly ever kept a preacher for more than a couple of years. Early in my ministry there I read *A Man Called Peter* by Catherine Marshall.[6] It is a wonderful book about the life, ministry, and untimely death of Peter Marshall. The book outlines the difficulty that often accompanies the second year of service in a church, and Dr. Marshall was no exception to that rule. I happened to be in my second year at the church in Melvin, Alabama when I read those words.

I made a decision that, with God's help, I would remain loyal to that church longer than the usual two years. We stayed there for a total of five years. Three sons were born there, many folks were married and buried while we were there, and my wife learned to cook biscuits and bake the bread she still makes for us there. One of the things I most look forward to in heaven is a reunion with some of the folks from that small, country church who have gone on before me.

Now I'm not saying, and the Bible does not say, that we should not work to improve our lives, to strengthen our muscles, or beautify our backyard. But there is an enormous wealth of joy in the heavenly places waiting for us in *loyalty* to the church, place, family, age, and job we have at this moment. Does it occur to us that we might just enjoy life more, not less, if we stay with one baseball team regardless of offers of millions more, or that there might be more satisfaction in staying with the spouse we have rather than trading for a younger model? Again, I am not saying nor does the Gospel of Jesus Christ require that we never change our circumstantial lives. But perhaps if we developed some of the contentment of Christ-centered values, we might find ourselves very rich, indeed, as we did in the heavenly places of Melvin United Methodist Church.

THE QUESTIONS AND SCRIPTURES

1. If your house was burning and you could only salvage five items, what would you choose?
2. If you were going to live one more year, what would you do? Would it be different than what you do now? Could you realistically alter your life to reflect the "one year" values?
3. What does God value most about you (for example, your work, your family, your love for Him and your family)?
4. What values leave you feeling trapped? What would be the smallest step toward the freedom God might want to give you (for example, trapped by your bills and income to pay them; freedom through a five-year plan to pay your debts and take the plunge to go back to school)?
5. What has brought you the greatest joy in your life? What will you do this month to cultivate that joy (for example, marrying my wife; date night every week!)?
6. What changes would enhance your commitment to Christ? What loyalties would enhance your commitment to Christ?
7. A hundred years from now, what might you wish you had done more, less, or differently? What can you do this month

to make yourself happier with your life values at that 100-year point?

8. Scripture for further reflection: Isa. 55; Matt. 6:19–33; John 10:1–30; 1 Tim. 6:2b–19; James 4:1–10, 5:1–6.

CHAPTER 9

CALLING: WHAT CAN I GIVE?

My wife, Calder, walked away from her nursing career on October 6, 2010. She'd had brain surgery about a year before, and had tried to return the health care work she so loved and in which she had flourished for thirty-five years. After several months of rehabilitation, she was cleared to attempt working again, and it seemed for a while that she would be able to continue.

The rigors of quality nursing service were extracting an increasingly high price, however. Her balance was compromised; the strength in her hands began to subside; her hearing was diminished; her legs lost strength; and she found it increasingly difficult to track and prioritize her patients' needs. The residual effects of the surgery and other health concerns made it increasingly apparent that she could not continue to provide good nursing care. The fact that I had been diagnosed with liver cancer added another stressor to the mix. And so, with tears of grief and a heart protesting against the loss of work, patients, and career she had so loved, she walked out of the hospital and away from her work in nursing for the last time.

But she had not left her calling.

Gradually, she began to realize that her calling was and is much bigger than just her work. She learned that the work may change, but the calling of God remains. That realization was as hard-earned as her nursing degrees had been in her younger years. Most of us, even those of us who, like Calder, have grown in Christ for years, tend to identify our work with our calling. It was only after hours of prayer and many conversations with her friends and me that she began to realize that calling and work are not the same.

The realization was practical at first. I simply needed her help, and that helped her realize that God was up to something good in her departure from hospital nursing. It was necessary, especially after I neared the top of the list for a liver transplant, for us to be near the University of Texas Medical Center in Dallas. The transplant surgery on January 28, 2011 was a wonderful gift, but the recovery was strenuous. I could not have safely accomplished that recovery and rehabilitation without Calder's help. I would not have had her help if she were still doing hospital work. Together, she and I began to see the cairns by the path toward her calling. The light grew brighter: God had not terminated her calling; he had changed the work that was part of that calling.

God taught us that His calling is much more than a job assignment. He calls us to love, live, grow, and work in a wide variety of forms. He calls us, above all, to Jesus Christ. He says to us, each day of our lives, what he said to his disciples throughout their lives: "Follow me" (Matt. 4:19; John 10:4, 12:26, 21:19). That is the call of God. That call is part of God loving us, loving through us, and shaping us into the likeness of Jesus Christ.

THE VALLEYS

There are two pervasive and destructive streams that flood the valley of our calling: the notion that *I am god of my calling* and the belief that *I am good through the work of my calling*. Os Guinness, in his wonderful and extensive work on this subject, *The Call*,[1] describes the temptations we face in our experience of God's call, and I have relied on his excellent perceptions as I developed this chapter.

"I am god of my call"

Christian people sometimes distort God's gifts, as we have seen in other dark and dysfunctional valleys of *Climbing Home*. How many times have you heard pastors, teachers at Christian schools, Christian businesspeople, fathers, wives, and many otherwise wonderful Christian people speak of *my* church, *my* class, *my* business, or *my* family? All of us have done that. And that's fine as a figure of speech. Sometimes though, "my" betrays an underlying belief. In actual fact, every realm, every good job, every family, every aspect of the call of God in our lives belongs to *him*. We are not gods of our calling.

It is important also that neither the church nor any of the church's ministers are gods of our calling. There is, to be sure, a place for the authority of the church and even the authority of the church's ministry. Jesus said not only to the apostles but to the church that serves in his name, "You will receive power when the Holy Spirit comes on you; and you will be my witnesses…" (Acts 1:8). The power of that witness is an authoritative power, but it is also always a derivative authority that is to be exercised in servant leadership, not spiritual dictatorship. Christian submission to the church and her ministers is not, therefore, submission to a dictator, but grateful reception of the service of Christ through the church and her ministers. Hebrews clarifies the place of church and ministerial authority:

> Have confidence in your leaders and submit to their authority, because they keep watch over you as those who must give an account. Do this so that their work will be a joy, not a burden, for that would be of no benefit to you. (Heb. 13:17)

I have many good friends who are part of denominations in which church and ministerial authority are emphasized. It is important, however, to keep in view that Jesus is Lord of our calling, not anybody in the church hierarchy.

Sometimes opinions in that hierarchy are intended positively but have a hurtful effect. I was the spiritual director of a wonderful retreat just before we moved to west Texas for doctoral work. It was a powerful time and many of the participants grew in Christ as a result of that retreat. I had said during the last day that my family and I would be going to another venue of service and ministry in west Texas, but that "Jesus Christ is the same yesterday and today and forever" (Heb. 13:8), and his work would continue and flourish. After that retreat, many lay people and ministers said they thought it was terrible that I was leaving the work of God in that community; some even said they hated my leaving the ministry. That stung. I realized with time that they meant well, but that their opinions could not define my calling as if they were gods.

Jesus was and is Lord of our calling.

The good news in this valley, however, is that if it is true that we are not gods of our calling, it is also true that the places where we work do not have the power to take our calling from us. We live in a world that is, perhaps justifiably, obsessed with jobs. And jobs are a part of calling. But the jobs we occupy are not the whole story. My wife found that her job as a nurse could depart along with her diminished strength, but her calling remained.

"I am good through my calling"

The loss of a job or the absence of any kind of work is a potentially significant blow to any person. This is often especially true of men; women find that homemaking sustains their self-esteem and significance, but men often feel that they are good and worthwhile only to the extent that they are gainfully employed.

In addition, as 1 Corinthians makes clear, we may excel at verbal, ideological, spiritual, and even sacrificial work, but if we are devoid of love, our work is worthless (see 1 Corinthians 13:1–3). If we believe we are *good through our calling* only, we can easily look down on others whose work we see as less significant than ours. We can consider ourselves superior to folks who have a smaller church or make less money or live in a smaller house or don't have as many degrees as we do. They must not be as good as we are. Paul spoke of this kind of vocational arrogance: "When they measure themselves by one another and compare themselves with one another, they are without understanding" (2 Cor. 10:12, ESV).

Many people fail to find work because they are looking for a job that will show how good they are. The call of God may well include work that is "menial;" that does not mean we are not good; it simply means our work is not a reflection of our value. Our value rests in the worth of Jesus Christ; he is the price of our calling. And because our value rests in him, we can be happy with a job like the tent-making of the apostle Paul (see Acts 18:3) or the fishing of Peter, James, and John (see Mark 1:16). One of our sons is a good example of someone with a very high sense of worth in his calling to follow Jesus Christ, although his jobs are "only" to work in a pizza business and a bakery.

If we feel we are good through our calling then we can also fall prey to a neglect of God's call for us to love our families, friends, and neighbors. Many professional people, ministers, businesspersons, professional athletes, and others consider that because their earnings and accomplishments make them good, it's OK that they don't spend much time with their families. But anyone who does this is not getting rich. They are getting poor, and so are their families. The isolation of work and the neglect of love robs them of the joy of the true call of God, the call to relationship.

THE PATHS

There are four cairns that lead forward to the heavenly places of God's call. These include a variety of stones that are helpful in understanding and pursuing this call. These cairns are: *the dimensions of calling, the expansion of God's call, the functions within calling,* and *church calling.*

Dimensions of Calling

The call of God is multidimensional because life is multidimensional. And that call revolves around the dominant relationships in our lives (to God, to ourselves, and to each other).

The word "call" in the New Testament is like words such as "grace," "hope," or "witness." These words are taken from everyday life and adopted into the vocabulary of God's kingdom. The two greatest commandments, to love God and to love our neighbor as ourselves, provide the pattern; our relationship with Jesus Christ is the center of all these and other major words of Christian life.

We are called primarily into a relationship with God in Jesus Christ. All of our work, witness, and worship flow from the call to this relationship. Jesus' last prayer, his prayer for you and me today, was a plea that God would make us one with him and each other as he is one with his Father. He said, "My prayer is…that all of them may be one, Father, just as you are in me and I am in you" (John 17:20,21). It is only as a result of that intimacy with God that "the world will know that you have sent me and have loved them even as you have loved me" (John 17:23). The witness and work of our calling is always and everywhere dependent on God's calling us into a relationship with himself.

This priority of our relationship with God over all our work for God is the only way we can make sense of some of the "everything," "always," and "in all things" statements of the New Testament. Paul says, "Whether you eat or drink or whatever you do, do it all for the glory of God" (1 Cor. 10:31); "Rejoice in the Lord always. I will say it again: Rejoice" (Phil. 4:4); "Whatever you do, whether in word or in deed, do it all in the name of the Lord Jesus…" (Col. 3:17); "Thanks be to God, who always leads us as captives in Christ's triumphal procession and uses us to spread the aroma of the knowledge of him everywhere" (2 Cor. 2:14); "If anyone is in Christ, the new creation has come: the old has gone, the new is here! All this is from God" (2 Cor. 5:17–18).

Those global statements make sense only because there is no place, no time, no activity, no job, no meal, no game, no conversation, and no part of life in which God is not calling us into relationships of love with himself and with each other. And if there is a behavior, attitude, relationship, or work where God is not welcome, we can be sure that we are at that point functioning outside the call of God.

When people walk, they don't normally skip steps. God says, "Walk in a manner worthy of the calling to which you have been called" (Eph. 4:1, ESV). The call of God encompasses each step you take in your life. In my late teens, a pastor told me concerning the overarching inclusiveness of God's call, "There is nothing secular with God; if you repair typewriters, teach fifth grade, rake leaves, write books, preach sermons, or cook pancakes, do it all as to the Lord, not to men."

Expansion of Calling

God calls us to love him, to love ourselves, and to love each other in very active ways. The focus of this call is relationships of love, and love is not static but active. God doesn't invite us to just sit around and think about how wonderful he is and to gaze into the eyes of our spouse. God does stuff in his love. And his call includes our doing stuff as well. Bob Goff has written a lively and spiritually-nourishing book, *Love Does*, which demonstrates the active quality of love and ways that behavior of love can transform our lives.[2] The action of God's call may change, however, while the central relationships remain the same. God often *expands our calling* and the ways he invites us to love him, ourselves, and each other.

I alluded in an earlier chapter to a very important conversation my wife and I had in our first pastoral appointment. Calder would often visit hospitals with me, as was the custom in South Alabama. But this one time she was caring for a sick child and so had stayed home. When I returned, she asked me how folks were doing. After I shared the progress of the hospitalized members of our community, she gave me one of those looks a wife can give when she knows her husband right well. She asked, sort of under her breath, "You really enjoy hospital and other visits, counseling, that sort of thing, don't you?"

I said, "I really do; I love supporting people that way."

She said, "You know, I wouldn't be surprised to see you go back to school in counseling one day."

I said, "Calder, I'll never leave the ministry; that's my calling." I had a pretty narrow view of calling in those days. Five years later I began doctoral work in counseling. I didn't leave my calling; God *expanded my calling*.

Function Within Calling

The primary *function* of God's call is to bring us to life in Jesus Christ, and the central feature of that life is active love for God, for ourselves, and for each other. The action that becomes part of our calling includes two primary functions: sustenance and service.

The opportunity to provide sustenance for those we love is rooted in God's creation and predates the entrance of sin into the world. God said to his first human beings, "Be fruitful and increase in number; fill the earth and subdue it" (Gen. 1:28). The provision of sustenance can take many forms and does not necessarily include a paycheck. I have often said in recent years that, as much as my wife and I enjoy eating out now and then, there is no restaurant in the whole state of Texas that has better bread than our own breakfast room table. Calder's bread doesn't pay like her nursing work did, but oh my, does it ever provide excellent sustenance!

Another *function within calling* is the provision of service to others. The thirteenth chapter of John's Gospel was one of my paternal grandfather's favorites in the Bible. He is the one who taught me that the head of a household, if he models his calling to lead his home after Jesus in that chapter, is called to be a household servant. We read that Jesus "having loved his own who were in the world…loved them unto the end" (John 13:1). Then the chapter gives an account of Jesus' washing the feet of the disciples. God calls parents of children and husbands of wives to seek out and provide service to those with whom they live in order to join God in his love for them.

Church Calling

We in the Western world live with a pretty individualistic mindset. God corrects that frame of mind in his calling to the Church—not just to individuals. The dimensions of God's call for the body of Christ are parallel to the dimensions of his call to individual believers in Christ. First and foremost God calls the Church to love for God, ourselves, and each other. Some of the action of that love takes place in a local church, and some can take place, as we discussed earlier, in a network of relationships beyond the local church.

The primary function of *church calling* is to nurture the members of the body of Christ that they may do the work of ministry and witness. Paul says that God gives various kinds of ministers to the Church,

> …to equip his people for works of service, so that the body of Christ may be built up until we all reach unity in the faith and in the knowledge of the Son of God and become mature, attaining the whole measure of the fullness of Christ. (Eph. 4:12–13)

This is one of the passages underlying the idea of the priesthood of all believers. Very simply, all Christians are called by God to love, relationship, provision, and service as part of the body of Christ. Frazer Memorial United Methodist Church is one of the places where this principle has been effectively implemented, as described in Dr. John Ed

Mathison's wonderful little book, *Every Member in Ministry.*[3]

The danger of church programs, as beloved as that aspect of service is to my Methodist soul, is that program busyness can take precedence over relationship with God, ourselves, and each other. It was a testimony to the spiritual strength and love in the first church I served that they were able to engage in a building program and maintain positive, loving relationships, though the process was a bit tense at times. Church programs can be effective, like family jobs that provide varieties of sustenance, only when they take place in the context of our calling to love God and our neighbors as ourselves. If a program facilitates and nurtures that love, it can be a significant cairn of church calling.

THE HEAVENLY PLACES

The heavenly places of life in Christ are not always grand, glorious, or great in the eyes of the world; but they are always fulfilling. No one experienced more joy or fulfilled his calling with more energy than the apostle Paul. And yet he was imprisoned four times, underwent a litany of sufferings (see 2 Cor. 11:23–33), and, according to generally accepted tradition, was not only abandoned by many of his friends (see 2 Tim. 4:10–16) but was eventually beheaded. Others have fulfilled the call of God, both to love God and others and to use their gifts to glorify him, and yet have had little notoriety in this world. As Os Guinness points out in *The Call,* someone who is as highly esteemed and treasured by the Christian community as Wolfgang Amadeus Mozart was buried in a pauper's grave, alone and unsung at the time of his death.[4] And yet there is nowhere an expression of the beauty and foretaste of the heavenly places in Christ Jesus any greater than the *Ave verum* from the requiem Mozart wrote as he was dying.

The call of God may not bring human glory but it does give God glory; and in giving God glory, his call can give us rest and joy. Jesus invited us:

> Come unto me, all you who are weary and burdened, and I will give you rest. Take my yoke upon you and learn from me, for I am gentle and humble in heart, and you will find rest for your

> souls. For my yoke is easy, and my burden is light. (Matt. 11:28–30)

God provides the rest we need. That rest is described in the epistle to the Hebrews and is foreshadowed by the land of Canaan in the Old Testament (see Hebrews 4:1–11). That land of Canaan is a portrayal of the heavenly places of milk, honey, rich abundance, and overflowing joy that is ours when God's call is fulfilled in us.

The heavenly places of God's call are not a bed of roses, but they are a beautiful garden of love, both divine and human.

Paul spoke of this ironic blend of earthly trouble and spiritual triumph in his own call:

> …through glory and dishonor, bad report and good report; genuine and yet regarded as imposters; known and yet regarded as unknown; dying, and yet we live on; beaten, and yet not killed; sorrowful, yet always rejoicing; poor, yet making many rich; having nothing, and yet possessing everything. (2 Cor. 6:8–10)

There is in Christ a paradoxical juxtaposition of the first being last, the last being first (see Mark 10:44), the weakness of Christ's death being the power of God to salvation (see 1 Corinthians 1:18), those who are faithful yet unrecognized being exalted to God's right hand (see Philippians 2:5–11), and those who humble themselves under the hand of God being lifted up (see 1 Peter 5:6).

There can be in this life of God's calling times when life is hard, even when life becomes fatal through disease, martyrdom, accident, or deterioration over time. The story of God's call is a story of endurance or perseverance and of triumph, even through all the difficulties life may throw at our calling. The biblical word for this endurance, this perseverance, is *steadfastness.* There can be trouble in the world, but we can be of good cheer, hearing Jesus say, "I have overcome the world!" The heavenly places are here—now—even in the world that he has overcome!

THE QUESTIONS AND SCRIPTURES

1. What do you fear you might lose if you let Jesus be Lord of your calling rather than keeping your own control of it? What might you gain?
2. What is the relation between your own work and your calling? What do you do to fulfill your calling at home? Does any of this need to change?
3. How could you help your local church fulfill God's call to love him, each other, and people in your community? How could you fulfill God's call in your extended church (family, friends, internet connections, past classmates, etc.)?
4. How could you more fully respond to God's call with your closest family and friends?
5. What could happen in your life this week if you respond to God's call more fully? How will you love him more fully, love yourself more productively, and love your spouse or closest friend in a more life-giving way?
6. Scripture for further reflection: Isa. 49:1–7; Jer. 1:4–10; Rom. 8:28–39; Eph. 4:1–13; 2 Pet. 1:3–11.

Chapter 10

PEACE: Will I be OK?

Guin, Alabama was destroyed in two minutes, from 7:50 PM to 7:52 PM, on April 3, 1974. I was working with the American Red Cross during that time, and on April 4 I was called into service for 36 hours of countywide damage assessment. The town lay in ruins when I arrived on scene; countywide, there had been 28 deaths, 272 injuries, and approximately $6,000,000 lost through property damage.[1] When I saw how completely the F5 tornado could destroy people's lives, I wondered, "How can there be peace in such a world?"

There was a man sitting on the crumpled back of an old, banged-up pickup truck; the windshield was busted out and the top crushed from being tossed about like a metal-clad rag doll. I knew my job was to categorize the property damage and move on, but an unseen hand drew me to that man's side. I sat on the crumpled truck with him. We were silent. In ten seconds, the winds of fury had dealt his world a devastating deathblow. Tears streamed quietly down his grizzled cheeks. Then, without a word or a sound, he very slowly lifted his arms toward heaven, and began to shake with sobs of grief. After a time of sitting, trembling in pain at the feet of Jesus, he looked at me with blue eyes that I shall never forget and said—stuttering, then babbling, then preaching Good News, "Bl… ble…b…bles…bles…blessed be…blessed be…blessed be the Name of…blessed be the Name of the Lord, blessed be the Name of the Lord, blessed be the Name of the Lord!" We talked of his granddaughter, killed by the storm, his wife who had passed on years before, his farm, and the chickens whose eggs he would never again bring to his breakfast table. And we both wept. Then he said, gazing into my soul with those red-rimmed blue eyes, "Son, don't feel sorry for me. The Lord has been with me through all of my seventy-two years, and he will carry me on home when it's time. You go on now; do your job, and don't worry for me. But, I can tell you're a praying man; pray for those who are alone."

What did he mean: "…those who are alone"? He sat by himself on his scrap of a truck; he was alone, wasn't he? And then I heard him; I really listened, and heard him.

I realized that his blue eyes were almost identical to my paternal grandfather's eyes, which had closed for his heavenward journey some five years before, my grandfather, who had lived just eleven miles from Guin. My grandfather, who had written, after my grandmother's death, on a postcard that I still keep treasured away in my Bible, "God is able, I know, to help me bear up under my load, and I am sure he is helping me every day." Then I understood what that old man had said; he was *not* alone. His faith, and the peace within his grief, stunned me.

How can there be peace in such a world? How did granddad have peace?

Well, God did give us a life with at least some predictability. We can rely on sunrise and sunset, the four seasons, reliable principles of gravity, cause and effect, that sort of thing. But God doesn't give certainty. In fact he says, "You do not even know what tomorrow will bring.… As it is, you boast in your arrogant schemes. All such boasting is evil" (James 4:14, 16).

The uncertainty of life, exemplified in that tornado, can lead to an anxious absence of peace, a valley of despair. Every minister, counselor, and teacher has seen life ripped apart in those we serve. It is not just big and dramatic destruction of life from that old man's tornado or granddad's loss of his wife of over sixty years, nor is it just major trauma like car wrecks or divorce or bankruptcy or cancer or any other of the "thousand natural shocks that flesh is heir to" (Shakespeare). It is also the erosion of life by the countless small events, conflicts, disappointments, weaknesses, and sins that leave us wondering, "How…? How can I have peace in my world?"

The need for peace is so far-reaching that it includes within itself all the other needs of *Climbing Home.* It includes the need for safety (see chapter on belonging), significance (see chapter on purpose), satisfaction (see chapter on resources), hope, and nearly every dimension of the gospel. It is not surprising that at the birth of salvation into the world, the angel herald came with the promise of peace (Luke 2:14). It is not surprising that at the departure from his earthly ministry Jesus' last word to the disciples was the promise of peace (John 14:27, 16:33). It is not surprising that Paul's letters to the young churches came with the greeting of peace (see Romans 1:7, 1 Corinthians 1:3, 2 Corinthians 1:2, Galatians 1:3, Ephesians 1:2, Philippians 1:2, etc.). Jesus Christ is the Prince of Peace (Isa. 9:6), and peace is the result of God's loving us into life and loving others through us.

Yet peace is so elusive. It is the quicksilver of the gospel, like the air we need to breathe but cannot control, and the water that we need to drink that slips through our fingers. So we construct spiritual and psychological aqueducts to try to dominate the flow of our badly-needed peace. We carve out the dysfunctional dark valleys in which we try to force peace and thereby destroy it.

THE VALLEYS

There are two canyons that reach far and deep into the valley of dysfunctional search for peace: *withdrawn living* and *defensive living*. These are so extensive in their reach that together they represent a bulk of the psychological pathology and of the sin described in the Bible. Our purpose here is to outline these canyons in order to find our way out of them.

Withdrawn Living

The search for peace through *withdrawn living* is similar to dealing with pain by flight. Many of us have, at one tumultuous time or another, had "desert island" or "cabin in the woods" fantasies. But it's not just hermits or castaways who live a withdrawn lifestyle. Most of us who seek peace through withdrawal do so under the rubric of one good activity or another. We are ministers, surgeons, teachers, homemakers, military officers, attorneys, sports fans, athletes, and some are writers who seek peace by means of a refreshing refuge.

It is important to make a distinction between withdrawing from life and a healthy lifestyle that includes places of refuge (see Psalm 46). A healthy refuge is something God can use to give us peace. We withdraw from life, on the other hand, because we have no peace. The same wilderness area or glass of wine or time of sexual intimacy can be a healthy refuge or an unhealthy escape. A healthy refuge helps us to engage in life refreshed; an unhealthy escape represents an avoidance of life.

Defensive Living

My wife and I grew up going to the woods and to the beach. She loves the beach very slightly more and I love the woods just a bit more. But we both loved each, and God used both to feed much of what we know of him. Both require good defensive strategies against some of the risks inherent in those wonderful places. It is important to know about things like undertow, falling rock, altitude, hypothermia, jellyfish, and wildlife. But the overprotectiveness of *defensive living* can prevent a person from ever going in the water or climbing a hill. *Defensive living* and *withdrawn living* share a characteristic in common: they can keep you from engaging in and enjoying the life God has for you.

This defensive lifestyle is particularly understandable, however, when life has not brought peace but rather injury. Hurricane Camille had a devastating effect on the Gulf Coast in 1969 and my family of origin saw many homes go from 50s bungalows constructed on the ground to fortresses built on stilts. In that situation, that kind of defensive construction makes sense. But others refused ever to build on the beach again, and that defense was understandable, too. Pain and tragedy can lead a person to both *withdrawn living* and a *defensive lifestyle* in order to prevent a repetition of trauma. For a similar reason, some folks said that we shouldn't go backpacking and mountain-climbing with my artificial hips.

A person who has been hurt in love may not want to build the trust to commit to a new relationship. Sometimes, even after marriage, a spouse who has been injured financially, spiritually, sexually, or in other ways may adopt a defensive lifestyle and try to build a relationship on stilts, as it were, maintaining a protective distance from areas of previous injury. Those elements of *defensive living* are most understandable, and I have spent the past twenty-five years of my career as a counselor helping folks to dismantle those very difficult walls.

Defensive living is not something to condemn, but something from which God provides liberation through his peace. His peace can give a person the freedom to risk a climb, a swim, a marriage, or even writing a book. The paths to that peace lead us to heavenly places of fully engaged, abundant life in Christ Jesus.

THE PATHS

The Prince of Peace invites us, "Follow me" (Matt. 4:19, John 21:19, see Isaiah 9:6). The acceptance of that invitation means we are on the path of peace. The whole journey of *Climbing Home* has been a map of that path, taking us out of the valleys that keep us away from that path and recognizing the heavenly places to which that path leads. That invitation from the Lord of Life is like one big cairn, the stones of which I have placed in this book. Three smaller cairns can help guide us on this path toward peace: *presence, providence,* and *perseverance.*

God's *presence* is the assurance that God's love accompanies us all the days of our lives; his *providence* is that activity of his love; *perseverance* is our response to that presence.

Presence

We left our camp at about 2:00 AM to come home. My wife and I had led a group on a backpacking trip to a base camp near Horn Fork Basin in the Collegiate Peaks Wilderness. Then she and I had set our little alarm for 1:00 AM to do something we had wanted to do for a long time: we wanted to climb Mount Harvard. We had made one previous attempt, and became stuck in an early fall whiteout; after we got soaked by the horizontal snow, we decided to make another attempt on another day. This was to be the day.

But one of our campers came to our tent as we were getting dressed to climb; she had developed a severe earache. We considered the alternatives, realized she was well beyond first aid, and reluctantly decided to pack up and walk out of the wilderness to take her to the doctor. All was well. We packed in about an hour and each had a headlamp to help follow the trail. One lady, however, was terrified by some things she had read about bears' nocturnal activity. She was literally whimpering as we proceeded, though she had been a trouper when we had climbed a mountain the day before. After a while, I turned around and said, "Sally Jo, I am right here; I'm going to be right in front of you; Calder is going to be right behind you; and Jesus himself is walking right beside you. We are with you. We will not leave you. We are right here, and we will be with you to the end of the trail. OK?" Then I prayed that Sally Jo's sense of God's presence would be so strong that she would have peace.

I did not promise a guarantee of her safety or that God would absolutely prevent any kind of mishap on the four miles back to the cars. Neither God nor I could or would provide a guarantee there were no bears in the woods; I knew better, both from experience and from the Bible. Christian ministers who promise something God does not give misrepresent real trust in him. I promised her *presence.* And that cairn was enough to give her peace.

Moses, Jeremiah, Peter, and all those who have followed Jesus Christ and have served him have walked that path, ever-aware of the dangers that lurk in the darkness. Moses stuttered, "Who am I that I should go to Pharaoh and bring the Israelites out of Egypt?" (Ex. 3:11). And God promised simply his presence: "I will be with you…" (Ex. 3:12). Jeremiah whimpered that he was too young to do what God asked of him, but God promised simply his presence: "Do not be afraid of them, for I am with you…." (Jer. 1:8). Jesus asked eleven disciples—eleven sinful men!—to make disciples of all nations—all nations!—promising, simply, presence: "Surely I am with you always, to the very end of the age" (Matt. 28:20). Jesus said he knew—he knew!—that after his departure, the disciples would experience all kinds of trouble (the word means pressure, stress) and promises, simply, presence: "I will not leave you as orphans; I will come to you" (John 14:18).

God can promise that he will be with us until he is blue in the face, but if we don't avail ourselves of that presence we can still be devoid of peace. There is a psalm that captures this practice of presence of God perfectly:

> O God, You are my God;
> Early will I seek You;
> My soul thirsts for You;

My flesh longs for You
In a dry and thirsty land
Where there is no water....
When I remember You on my bed,
I meditate on You in the night watches....
My soul follows close behind You;
Your right hand upholds me. (Ps. 63:1, 6, 8, NKJV)

Providence

Providence is one of those words, like "character" or "humor," which is not used much in the Bible yet reflects biblical principles. The word translated *providence* means literally "to see or to know beforehand," and refers to God's going ahead of our lives to provide what is needed at our various stages of development and circumstance.

The meaning that emerges out of Reformed theology focuses on God's sovereign direction or control of life, even in its difficulties, for the good of his people. A related understanding is focused more on God's allowing events of human life for our growth and benefit. The emphasis on control is more oriented around God's direction of what happens; the emphasis on permission is more oriented around God's creating good from what happens. One of my sons expressed a blended view in a master's thesis in history: "God used all things in life and history for his glory and the spiritual benefit of his people."[2] A part of that providential work may include control of human life, but it is the clear message of the Bible that providence is primarily a matter of God's providing his presence, wisdom, and direction to create good out of all the events and circumstances of life.

God is present in many ways to provide for our good and also our peace. He says, "Never will I leave you; never will I forsake you" (Heb. 13:5). God said to Moses when he was terrified at the prospect of leading God's people toward the land of promise, "My presence will go with you, and I will give you rest" (Ex. 33:14). Furthermore, God assures us that he will effectively love us into life by conformity with the image of Jesus Christ: "In all things God works for the good of those who love him, who have been called according to his purpose…to be conformed to the image of his Son" (Rom. 8:28–29). God also promises that he will exercise his power to preserve our life in Christ. Jesus says of us, "I give them eternal life, and they shall never perish; no one will snatch them out of my hand" (John 10:28).

God's love for us is immutable, unchanging, and triumphant. Paul says,

> I am convinced that neither death nor life, neither angels nor demons, neither the present nor the future, nor any powers, neither height nor depth, nor anything else in all creation, will be able to separate us from the love of God that is in Christ Jesus our Lord. (Rom. 8:38–39)

That is the promise of God's providence. This is what he promises to his people even in the midst of exile, "I know the plans I have for you, …plans to prosper you and not to harm you, plans to give you hope and a future" (Jer. 29:11).

That is peace.

Perseverance

The *presence* of God and the *providential* assurance that he will bring good to our lives assure the *perseverance* of our life in Christ.

Now, of course, being a retired United Methodist minister, I know that Christians can fall from grace. My goodness, I have fallen from grace. But God does *not* fall from grace! Paul says, "He who began a good work in you will carry it on to completion until the day of Jesus Christ" (Phil. 1:6). He later says, "It is God who works in you to will and to act in order to fulfill his good purpose" (Phil. 2:13).

I worried as a child, as many of us do, that some kind of trouble would ruin my life. Little girls worry that they won't be pretty enough, boys that they won't be tough enough, Christians that they won't be good enough. We live with anxiety that our inadequacies will doom us to unhappy lives. Well I did manage to get myself into a passel of trouble, as many of us do. But God's grace was and is greater than all my troubled life. He has brought me out, and he can bring you out to a place of peace and joy and gladness. As the psalmist said,

> God…has preserved our lives
> and kept our feet from slipping.
> For you, God, tested us;
> you refined us like silver.
> You brought us into prison
> and laid burdens on our backs.
> You let people ride over our heads;
> we went through fire and water,
> but you brought us to a place of abundance. (Ps. 66:8–12)

Jesus Christ is the Savior, not only of our souls, but of our whole lives. Jesus "is able to save completely those who come to God through him" (Heb. 7:25). The gracious *perseverance* of his work to save and love and enjoy us means that he is, he really is, *for* us—even with all of our falling away then turning back to God again, the Prince of Peace.

THE HEAVENLY PLACES

When we see Jesus, we see peace. There are two somewhat different places where he appears in our lives to bring peace: *confidence* and *nature*. There are countless other places where the peace of God appears is our lives, some of which we have discussed, such as communion, devotional living, and hope. The *confidence* that is ours in Christ and the promise of peace that often appears in *nature* can bring us solace in our often troubled world.

Confidence

Have you ever known anyone with a quiet, assured, and attractive *confidence*? When it derives from Jesus Christ, *confidence* is not a brash, boastful thing but carries within its spirit the humility and grace of its source. The assurance of God's perpetual grace and love can give both an awareness of the potential for trouble around us and yet an answer to the question of peace: life in Jesus Christ will be OK.

The book and life of Esther provide a good example of this kind of *confidence.* You may recall that the book has been the subject of occasional debate as to its canonicity and the validity of its message due to both some of its content and deficiencies. For example, the name of God is not mentioned, and the book has considerable violence. But just as God's name is not often mentioned positively in the modern public square, his presence, purpose, and providential action are present nonetheless. The book represents a significant part of the historical Jewish feast of Purim, which celebrates the perseverance of God's covenant people in spite of the violent threat that could have annihilated them.

That perseverance and the feast of Purim came as result of Esther's courageous *confidence* and consequent willingness to risk her life for the people of God. An order had been given in the name of King Ahasuerus to kill all of the Jews and to plunder their goods. Esther, who had achieved favor with the king although she was a Jew, received word of that order and became quite concerned for her people. She knew the cultural rule that if she went in to the king to intercede for her people, she might well be killed. After asking that prayers and fasting take place on her behalf, she said, "When this is done, I will go to the king, even though it is against the law. And if I perish, I perish" (Esther 4:16).

This calls to mind the courageous *confidence* of another woman of God. Mary knew the dangers of being found pregnant (by the Holy Spirit, no less) before she was married to Joseph; but she said, "Let it be to me according to your word" (Luke 1:38, NKJV). That is the *confidence* of the peace of God.

Nature

God speaks through nature in some interesting ways, ways that show the heavenly places of peace may be closer than we think. Years ago, I would occasionally watch children's TV shows with my boys. We would discuss what we had seen and then we would talk about our neighborhood, wilderness, what makes a wonderful day, justice, the peculiarities of the number 8, their favorite things, or the way a flower can grow. Once on one of their shows there was a beautiful close-up picture of a jonquil with a drop of dew on it. A piece of classical music played softly as the dew slowly, gently rolled down the sunlit petal. It was a springtime picture of God's presence. The music neared its quiet end and the camera panned out until, just as the drop of moisture fell to the ground, we saw that the jonquil was growing beside a garbage can in an alley surrounded by dilapidated buildings and draping clotheslines. God's creation can bring his peace to the most unexpected places.

We have been most blessed in our family to have lived for years with a love of nature. Nature can, of course, be just the opposite of peaceful. We have seen Gulf of Mexico storms that were terrifying, and we always tried to begin a mountain climb a great while before daylight in order to avoid the terrible lightening that often accompanies afternoon thunderstorms. But the world of God's creation often provides a window on the beauty of holiness, the splendor of peace at the feet of Jesus. Sometimes all we need do is look, listen, and respond to God's invitation (see Psalm 46:10).

I have seen visions and still dream dreams of the peace of God in the heavenly places of the earth: the picture of a gentle mountain rain falling off the poncho of one of my dearest friends as he stood beholding the kindness of God to the earth, the view from the peak of a fourteen-thousand-foot mountain, the soft cooing and babbling of a small mountain stream, the stillness of a quiet snowfall filling our yard and the park across the road with white purity (calling to mind the blood of Jesus that has washed us white as snow), and the power of a small blue columbine, rising out of earth that was dead with winter just weeks before, painted by the hand of the one who whispered a Word and planted wildflowers and then flung the stars across the sky:

> The heavens declare the glory of God;
> the skies proclaim the work of his hands.
> Day after day they pour forth speech;
> night after night they reveal knowledge.
> …their voice goes out into all the earth,
> their words to the ends of the world. (Ps. 19:1–2, 4)

Those heavens, those skies, the wonder of those days and nights, and the echoes of those voices of nature all around us, they are the picture of the heavenly places of peace in Christ Jesus.

THE QUESTIONS AND SCRIPTURES

1. What are some of the areas that cause you the greatest anxiety? How do you cope with those anxieties? It that working for you? What alternatives are there to give you peace in place of anxiety?
2. How much difference is there between the peace you experience in everyday life and the peace you have when you get away? How could the peace in your places of refuge translate to your daily life?
3. What are five ways you could increase your sense of the presence of God (for example, walk your dog, thank God every hour, on the hour, for what he is doing, ask God with each person you meet how God would like to love that person through you)?
4. Spend five minutes five days in a row looking at something beautiful in nature.
5. What aspects of *Climbing Home* could bring you more peace with God, with yourself, with those closest to you (for example, defining yourself as God defines you, developing more of a sense of God's grace, allowing your expectations to be replaced by the hope that God gives, nurturing your love for yourself in ways consistent with God's love for you)?
6. Scripture for further reflection: Ps. 46, 63, 66; John 14–17; Col. 3:15–17; Phil. 4:4–19.

Part III
Questions of Hope

My student had a crippling and, as it turned out, terminal disease. He was a most attractive person, extremely bright, the apple of his parents' eyes, and one of the stars of the department in which he was a scholarship student at Texas Tech University. His parents were wonderful Christian people. They became courageous in the face of their son's illness, praying for his healing, recognizing that God heals sometimes by removing a disease, sometimes through medical procedures, and sometimes by ushering one of his children gently into heaven.

Then these parents and their son began to follow a religious group that assured them of a long and prosperous life for their son if they would follow a particular set of rituals and pray a particular way. They quit going to their counselor, stopped attending the Baptist church where they had been faithful for generations, abandoned the medical regimen that had looked at least somewhat promising, and promised each other that he would not only survive but would thrive. For God willed it so.

But that young man died. The family blamed God for letting them down, for betraying them, for failing to keep his promise.

They had been so hopeful.

"Hope springs eternal in the human breast," according to Alexander Pope.[1] The human drive toward hope is a positive source of energy for the growth and improvement of life. The anecdote concerning my student illustrates the importance of having hope that is based on well-founded expectations.

The effect of unbiblical, unwarranted hope is devastating. What if Paul had lived in hope that his discipleship to Jesus Christ would protect him from prison, shipwreck, whipping, or rejection (even by the Christian community)? What if the early martyrs had lived in hope that since God protected Daniel from the lions, he would keep them from losing their lives in the Roman coliseum? What if Jesus had agreed with Peter's initial reaction to the prediction that the Messiah would be crucified? "Never, Lord!… This shall never happen to you" (Matt. 16:22). Jesus' response to Peter was quick and definite: "Get behind me, Satan! You are a stumbling block to me; you do not have in mind the concerns of God, but merely human concerns" (Matt. 16:23). False hope destroys true hope.

The entire Christian enterprise depends on the people of God living by faith in the truth, hope in the way, and love for the life that God gives. We cannot live healthy spiritual lives if we fabricate our faith from illusions, our love from what we want rather than need, or our hope out of wishful thinking ("hope springs eternal….").

These next five chapters attempt to spell out the biblical promise of hope by responding to some of our basic questions. How can we cope with the pain of the family in the above story? What is the place of pleasure in the life of Christian people? What does the gospel of Jesus Christ hold out as a realistic hope for God's people in light of the limited resources with which many people live? The goal of these pages is freedom from false hopes that leave us disappointed and angry at God, and I will describe cairns that point the way toward good hope, authentic pictures of life in the heavenly places of hope.

Chapter 11

HOPE: What can I expect?

I called at about 2:00 AM, October 10, 1976. My wife had given me a liter of Johnny Walker Black Label scotch, a case of Budweiser, and two bottles of Boone's Farm apple wine on Friday afternoon. She had hoped I would, this time, make it last if she gave me some of "the good stuff" she knew I liked. She and I kept trying the same thing, hoping for a different result. But the result was always the same. I was functional—didn't miss work and paid the bills. But I always wound up drunk at night, trembling in the morning, miserable throughout the day until I could begin to drink again. I was an alcoholic. I was hopeless. I was hopeless until I learned by the grace of God to say what I still say today.

I'm Madoc. And I am an alcoholic.

When I called Alcoholics Anonymous, I began to learn to say that. When I gave up hope of saving myself from the ravages of alcoholism, I began to have hope that God could do what I could not do. The sponsor known to me simply as "Buck" called back from the answering service of Alcoholics Anonymous and, with no judgment or moralizing or excusing, he simply joined me in the gutter of my slurred-speech, desperate existence. This man, who was obviously sober said, "It sounds to me like you and I have a lot in common." He was an instrument of grace. And grace gave me hope.

It took years to approach anything like consistent sobriety. My "slips" taught me the cunning, baffling, powerful nature not only of alcoholism, but of the lure of hopeless and sinful life in general. Sobriety of any kind—a life of abiding hope—lies at the end of a long climb for any of us. It takes so long and is so hard to come by because we are so persistently hopeful for the wrong things; we so stubbornly resist surrendering our false hope that it takes a long time to achieve true hope in

Jesus Christ. Even after many years of sobriety, I still stand amazed at the stunning craftiness of sin to lure me back into the valley of hopelessness.

I went into inpatient treatment to try to break the stranglehold of my addiction. I thank God to this day for that ministry. One of the first elements of the healing process was an answer to a simple question. The intake counselor said that many patients answered this question with long, rambling explanations, but she requested as simple an answer as I could give. She asked, "Why do you drink?" I did not need a sentence or a paragraph; I needed only one word: "Fear. I drink because of my fear."

Fear creates a relentless quest for hope, any hope that life will be good and that our fears will not be realized. An infant can see his or her mother walk across the room and be seized by a terror that Mama has gone away never to return. Every mother knows the sound of the shriek that follows that fear. It's far from a wet diaper, hungry, tired, or colicky cry; it's the wail that life will not be good because the source of life is leaving.

From those early moments on, we cry out desperately for hope that life will be good. And we try. Oh, we try everything to guarantee that our fears will not be realized, that we will be protected and propped up and provided with the good stuff we so crave.

We cling desperately to whatever promises to help us realize our hopes. That's why I held so tenaciously to alcohol. For when I was drinking, I was not afraid. I was hopeful. Life would be good because I felt good, and I was surely ten feet tall and bulletproof. I was terrified of leaving that feeling. I wanted so badly to be a "successful" drinker that I even learned to control my drinking to some extent. It's that way with all functional alcoholics, or gambling addicts, or those with secret addictions to work, pornography, control, violence, power, or religion.

Out of our fear that life will not be good, we cling to fragile expectations—any illusion, any marriage, any church, any job, any substance, any power, or anything else good or bad that promises assurance. That is the power behind idolatry. We may wonder why anyone in their right mind would believe in the idols of sun or moon…or wealth or alcohol.

Stupid, isn't it? But it comes from desperation. Like mountain-climbers who are falling, we lay hold of the nearest precarious branch out of the desperate fear of losing our lives, but then those branches break and send us tumbling to our death.

Once Calder and I were climbing Notch Mountain in Colorado. We had our dog Tara with us. It's a nice hill that provides a splendid view of the Mount of the Holy Cross, which at the right time in the early summer has a clearly outlined cross of snow on its south face. The climb up Notch is not at all difficult, just a bit long. But Calder slipped. She slid over the edge of the trail and was grasping at the dry, bare earth for a handhold to keep her from falling over a ledge of about thirty feet. I yelled in fear, "Calder, quit trying to hold on and just lie still!" I inched my way down to her, digging my boots into the earth to provide adequate purchase for leverage, telling her not to lift her hand or try to climb up. I reached out for her hand with one of mine, boots dug in, holding a sapling with my other hand, and pulled her up. It was frightening.

Desperate hope could have killed her if she had kept clawing at the ground, because she would have slid further down the hill and nothing would have prevented her fall to the ledge below. Do you see how it works sometimes? Hope can kill faith. God's Name is never taken in vain as surely as when it is used to promise something that he does not grant in his Word. The goal of this chapter is to explore the hope that is grounded in God's Word and gives assurance that life will be good in Jesus Christ.

THE VALLEYS

The valley of hopelessness is a dark place. Yet somehow those who dwell there don't try to escape. The valley holds tightly to its occupants with threats: "If you leave this place, you will lose everything you value!" Multiple chains keep us bound in this valley: denial, compulsive dependence, an absolute conviction that we can create our own hope right there in the valley, false hope in a person, a cult, a training program, perhaps to the magic of changing from bourbon to beer.

We are pitifully like the rich young ruler in Jesus' parable (see Luke 18:18–23), who held to his self-lived life rather than receiving the grace of God. It was a hope issue. That young man, like all of us, needed hope of eternal life. Jesus immediately went to the heart of the matter and showed the man that he would have to relinquish his hope in wealth in order to receive the freely-given hope of all the wealth of the kingdom of God. His response is our response. When Jesus offers us the riches of life, of joy, of pleasure, of courage to cope with pain, and a life centered in the true treasures of God's presence, we go away sorrowful. Rather than receiving the wealth of God, we would rather hold onto the riches of our power, our religious self-righteousness, our alcohol, our winning at sports, our business, our gambling thrills, our sexual excesses, and our sin.

At least two chains bind us in this valley of hopelessness: *denial* and *determination.*

Denial

Denial is not, as we say in Alcoholics Anonymous, the name of a river in Egypt. It is the dynamic power that prevents the possibility of hope in Christ. For the heart of denial is belief that rather than being a problem, our alcohol, gambling, work, money, sexual behavior, control, or quest for others' approval is the solution to our need for hope.

This belief is never so strong as when it comes from religious conviction. Ministers and Christian counselors have seen many people who maintain an addictive hold on their idols of hope, sometimes claiming that they are gifts of the Spirit; they refuse to let go and let God be God!

Sometimes we deny the destructiveness of our idols because they are good gifts used in addictive ways. I have seen my wife, my mother, and others drink a glass of wine and thank God for it. I myself can eat three bites of dark chocolate ice cream drizzled with hot fudge and do so with gratitude; the wine or the ice cream are not in themselves the addiction; the addiction is in our idolatrous use of the wine or dessert. The same is true of work, or money, or church, or the approval of others. When the good gifts of God replace God himself, they become destructive, life-draining idols.

Precisely because these are good things, it is easy to deny their idolatrous power to chain us to the valley of hopelessness. Our denial keeps us terrified of letting go and following Jesus Christ up the path toward true hope.

Determination

I became determined to prove that I could drink "normally." I read in The Big Book of Alcoholics Anonymous that if someone isn't sure about being an alcoholic, let him try some controlled drinking.[1] So I tried. And I tried some more. When that didn't work out so well, I tried just a little bit harder. I even invoked the name of my paternal grandfather and his North Alabama strong will. He had been able to survive the Depression with five children. If he could feed those children every two weeks with just one five-pound sack of flour, surely I could take a sip of bourbon or drink a beer with barbecue. So I tried some more.

The root of my *determination* was my idolatry of self. Such arrogance can blind us to the truth of God and feed our defiant determination to prove that we can live successfully in the valley of addictive idolatry. We believe that other people may have problems misusing the gifts of God, but we are so very determined to follow Christ in our controlled use of his gifts.

THE PATHS

My life of addictive, idolatrous bondage left me gasping for breath in the valley of hopelessness. "God help me!" I cried. Hopelessness is such a dark place that all we can do is cry out. When my recovery from alcoholism was in its early and inconsistent days, I would often go to a church where I knew I could be alone. I would sit and grasp the pew in front of me and pray over and over and over again my mantra for hope, "God, heal me from within."

But I found that the path forward to the heavenly places of sobriety passes by three cairns that can bring pause to our prayers. They make us wonder, "Do I really want to leave this valley?" The three cairns, unappealing at first glance, run counter to our natures and can lead us to retreat back to the bravado of determined denial. These three cairns are *surrender, support,* and a lifelong *search* for growth into Christ in all things.

Not only do these cairns lead us forward out of addictions such as alcoholism, they also lead us out of many other forms of hopelessness that are addictive. It may be a woman's obsession with being thin, a teenager's cutting, a man's compulsion to get his golf score below 80, or a minister's drive to have his church reach a certain membership. These and many other forms of drivenness leave us in despair, because we had so hoped that these pursuits would bring us happiness. And, thinking we know better than God, it's hard to let go. Repentance is never easy, but for some of us it is necessary for life to become extremely hard, for us to reach a bottom, in order to move forward.

However, if we take a look at the path forward and the heavenly places of hope at the summit; we may just decide it's worth the effort to go *Climbing Home* out of the valley of hopelessness.

Surrender

Surrender is indeed unappealing to our egotistical desire to do life our way. But the word means something quite different in a biblical context. The word is *parhistemi* and the root meaning in Romans 6:13 and 12:1 has to do with presenting yourself for service, like a soldier presenting himself for military service, ready to both sacrifice and obey for the sake of the mission.

The New King James translation is therefore quite accurate: "Present yourselves to God as being alive from the dead" (Rom. 6:13). The term *surrender* may seem to convey the idea of giving up in a battle, handing over the sword to the conqueror. And there may be an element of that in the battle between us and God. In fact many passages of the Bible make it clear that God loves us in spite of our sinful predisposition to enmity with him (see, for example, Romans 5:10). But *surrender* as a cairn pointing to the heavenly places of hope is primarily a matter of presenting ourselves to God in such a way that he can work his life, love, and will in us.

The thoughts and writings of a seventeenth-century Carmelite lay brother fondly known as Brother Lawrence express this concept well. The theme of Brother Lawrence's ministry is *The Practice of the Presence of God*, and his writings have been reissued many times.[2] The focus of this simple man's message is that God is present in all of life for a

Christian and that living in the ambience of God's love transforms even the most ordinary details of life into an arena for the glory and enjoyment of God. Surrender, then, is like holding out our plate to be filled in a buffet line. We choose to present our lives to God so that he can fill us with his loving Spirit.

Surrender as life in God's continual presence becomes the foundation of hope. We worry about what we can expect from life because we need to know that life will be good, but life carried out in God's presence can be nothing but good. I was seeking an assurance of good rather than the realization of childhood fears when I abused alcohol in order to feel "ten feet tall and bulletproof." Of course it didn't work. None of the solutions of the valley work. They give anguish and despair instead of hope.

But surrender—the choice to live all of life in the presence of God––does give hope. With God, life will be good even when it is difficult. For God is with us. God is for us. "If God is for us, who can be against us?" (Rom. 8:31).

Support

We need more than the presence of God alone, however; we need *support* from other people. I have a lump of charcoal in my office that came from a spiritual retreat many years ago. Beside the lump of charcoal is a lump of coal from near my grandfather's house in north Alabama. Each reminds me of the warmth of relationship. If a source of heat is isolated from a flame, it will not catch fire; if it is isolated from oxygen, the fire will not continue; if isolated from other sources of combustion, the fire will go out. Those pieces of charcoal and coal are metaphors reminding me that God's people need each other as well as God.

All of us need ministry from others. Some need counseling, some devotional aids, some teaching of theology, some just need a listening ear or a warm smile or a good laugh. But we all need each other and all those around us need our ministry as well.

That means we need church. It may take time to find a place we feel we truly belong. It may take experimentation to find a place where we feel Jesus Christ is lifted up and his Spirit nurtures our lives. Church for many of us may include many people from many different places with whom we share ministry via the Internet, in a Bible study, over the phone, or in other venues in addition to traditional church services. There are many denominational and non-denominational resources available to Christian people today. Some may prefer more ritual, some a "happy-clappy" style, and others a more theologically focused ministry. But each of us needs shared ministry, and that means each of us needs church.

When hope is tested by the vicissitudes of life, as it often is, then especially we need each other. Some of the times when we most need shared ministry may be times when it is difficult to reach out to others. Pain tends to be embarrassing and therefore isolating. We do our best to keep from crying in public. When I began to realize in seminary that I had some serious issues for which I needed counseling, I literally poured over Karen Horney's book *Self Analysis*, hoping that I could be my own counselor and avoid the embarrassment of asking for help.[3] I especially felt that way concerning asking for help with alcoholism. My goodness, I had (I thought) surrendered to Christ, had entered the ministry, and had by that time gone to years of counseling; surely I didn't need help with my alcoholism. But I did.

We all do. We don't all need help with the same thing, but we all need each other. We all need help with something. If we want to live lives of hope, to have an assurance that life will be good, we will acknowledge the cairn of support and reach out to both help and be helped.

Search

The church, or place of shared ministry and support, is designed by God to be a place where we can *search* to grow up into Christ in all things. Christians love to say, and rightly so, that we are saved. But John Wesley actually got it right when he said that salvation is a threefold process: we have been saved, we are being saved, and we will be saved at the consummation of the kingdom of God in the coming of Christ.[4] Jesus Christ lives in us (see Galatians 2:20) and he is working in us, "both to will and to act in order for you to fulfill his good purpose" (Phil. 2:13). These and many other passages make it clear that salvation does not end with our initial faith in Christ. Faith in Christ as our Savior is the beginning of a search to grow up into him in all things (see Ephesians 4:15).

People of Reformed tradition (and others as well) see salvation as an ongoing experience of glorifying God and enjoying him forever.[5] The present, active quality of seeking to become increasingly like Jesus Christ is not an attempt to gain a holier-than-thou kind of status in relation to others. It is a growth orientation of life, and it gives hope a new meaning.

Hope is no longer a matter of gaining the fulfillment of a wish list of stuff; it is a matter of moving forward toward conformity with Jesus Christ. This hope can affect the bad times as well as the good times, perhaps especially the bad times. For our hope in Christ is the most fully realized and the most powerful to transform all of life into an arena of good when that hope triumphs over hopelessness. Then hope brings about the growth of Christ in our lives precisely when we might expect life to be defeated (see Colossians 1:27).

The covenant of God with his people is the context of this search to grow up into Christ in all things. The covenant formula in the Bible is simple, but far-reaching: "I will be their God, and they will be my people" (Heb. 8:10). This covenant promise, or God's agreement to be with us in lives of continual hope, does not guarantee that he will prevent all disease, disaster, or human dereliction; he promises that he will be our God, and we will be his people, period!

There will be no power, no calamity, no sin, no suffering, nothing present, nothing to come, nothing in the whole wide world that can separate us from God as our God and the working of his love in us as his people (see Romans 8:38–39). That means that there is no time when we cannot seek him who made the seven stars and Orion (see Amos 5:8), no time when we cannot seek him who spoke a word and flung the stars across the night sky, no time when we cannot seek him in whose birth are met all the hopes and fears of all the years,[6] and no time when we cannot seek and learn of Jesus Christ and so find rest for our souls (see Matthew 11:29). There is no time, no time that cannot be a time of hope.

THE HEAVENLY PLACES

The heavenly places of life in hope are characterized by lives of *sobriety* and *serenity.* Our hope in Christ is far from the guarantee of an easy life.

These qualities can fill us with abiding hope even when facing the mouths of lions, the rejection of friends, the deficiencies of economic hardship, the ravages of disease, or any of the other difficulties of life.

Sobriety

An excavation of the biblical word for sobriety reveals a meaning of "sensible, realistic, sound-minded." We had an expression at the churches I served in south Alabama for a person who was drunk and acting crazy; we'd say, "He just ain't at hisself." I would often think of that expression when reading the parable of the prodigal son (Luke 15:11–32). The youngest son of a family decided to leave home and go spend his inheritance in wild and wanton waste. He eventually succumbed to the destructiveness of his lifestyle and came to a time of depravation, hunger, and desperate need. But we read that "…when he came to himself…" (Luke 15:17, NKJV) he began the journey back home. He began *Climbing Home.*

The return of the prodigal clearly shows how the sobriety of the Bible is not at all a long-faced thing. The prodigal went home to a party, thrown by his father in joy that his son had finished the climb back into the fold. The sobriety that God gives includes celebration of all the good gifts God gives.

"Sobriety" does not just refer to alcoholism or other addictions. A person can become drunk on any of the good things of life: education, family, power, work, politics, church, play, houses, goods, kindred, as well as alcohol. I know.

I became addicted to my ministry at one point in my life. One Saturday night I was still visiting church members at 9 PM. There's nothing wrong with working late or working hard, and if there had been an emergency or a church meeting my returning home late would have been understandable. But it had become a pattern. I had, as alcoholics often do, switched addictions. I was obsessed with ministry. It became almost as painful, though more subtle, as my former addiction to alcohol. I had to learn that sobriety in the heavenly places of hope is largely an issue of enjoying the gifts of God in perspective, in light of the supremacy of Jesus Christ in all things.

It was in relation to ministry that Paul said, "I say…to every one of you: Do not think of yourself more highly than you ought, but rather think of yourself with sober judgment…" (Rom. 12:3). That sobriety of self-assessment can undergird a lifestyle of sobriety.

Serenity

The heavenly places of hope include two elements of *serenity*. First, the serenity of hope brings a comfortable confidence that life will be good. Several years ago William Glasser wrote a briefly popular book entitled *Schools without Failure.*[7] We aren't going to debate the pedagogical effectiveness of Glasser's work here, but the book raises an interesting question. What would your life be like if you could know that, regardless of the challenges you faced, your life would be good? That is the confidence of hope we can have in Jesus Christ. We can know that even when our circumstances are bad, life can be good if it is held in the gentle but powerful hands of God.

Second, the serenity of hope in Christ can give humor. Humor without hope is cruel. I occasionally laugh at the awkwardness of walking with the artificial hips I was surgically given in 1979. Some might find that cynical, some courageous; others would wonder why I would laugh at something as difficult as a crippled-up gait. But hope in Christ enables me to chuckle about that infirmity. I can't run but I can walk. So my wife and I have backpacked, hiked, and climbed about 1200 miles in the past thirty or so years. Although we don't do as much outdoor stuff as we once did, I can laugh at my awkwardness, remembering the time when I was a "lean, mean, climbin' machine," and looking forward to a time when I will again climb all over my new home with Jesus. When that hope wells up inside me, the awkwardness of my walking around the heavenly places of this earth can bring a smile rather than a tear. I laugh, with hope in Christ.

THE QUESTIONS AND SCRIPTURES

1. What hopes have left you disappointed? Where did those hopes come from? How did you deal with the disappointment?

2. How do you feel about the statement that "life will be good in Jesus Christ?" Angry, confused, resentful, sad? How would a change in your understanding of hope change your response?
3. Read John 14–16. What does Jesus promise to give that can assure you that your life will be good?
4. What people have provided you the most support in maintaining a positive, hopeful attitude toward life? How did their support help you during a difficult time?
5. What people have you supported in maintaining a positive, hopeful attitude toward life? How have you supported them during a difficult time?
6. What people, behaviors, or substances are you counting on to give you good life? Are they reliable? Does your hope create pressure for those people or behaviors? Could you enjoy those people, behaviors, or substances more if they didn't carry the load of all your hope?
7. Are there ways in which you need to relinquish some of your hopes in order to live by hope in Christ alone?
8. Scripture for further reflection: Jer. 29:4–14, 31:30–37; Isa. 60–62; Luke 15:1–32; Rom. 8:1–39; 1 Pet. 1:3–9.

Chapter 12

RESOURCES: Will I have enough?

We took a ton of stuff the first time our family went backpacking. We had been camping for several years, and had backpacked overnight a couple of times, but this was our first time to carry a few days' supplies on our backs. We were going into the Cruces Basin Wilderness in northern New Mexico, and we wanted to be sure we had all we needed. My goodness, were we ever loaded. We had frying pans, a heavy stove, enough rope to hog-tie a herd of cattle, and lanterns of all kinds. I even packed a surprise: a tape recorder with some of our favorite tunes on a cassette tape! I was carrying forty-nine pounds, my wife thirty-nine pounds, and our boys had an elephant on their backs! Our oldest was ten and the twins were eight, and they had between twenty-five and thirty pounds each. I heard them grunt a few times, trying to hide the pain, and knew I had packed too much. I had wanted to be sure we would have enough.

Just imagine the anxiety of the whole nation of Israel, embarking on a wilderness journey of unknown duration and destination, asking, "Will we have enough?" It didn't take long before they complained that Moses had not adequately prepared. They said to Moses, "If only we had died by the hand of the Lord in Egypt! There we…ate all the food we wanted. But you have brought us out into this desert to starve this assembly to death" (Ex. 16:3). And then when God provided manna to provide sufficient nutrition for the journey, they complained that it wasn't enough. They would like quail (under glass?) please (see Numbers 11:4–6).

These two stories illustrate one of the challenges in answering the question, "Will I have enough?" There is an underlying question: what *is* enough to meet my needs? How far ahead should I assure the supply of my needs in order to have the safety I need? Do I really need a full freezer and bank account in order to feel safe?

My wife and I went on our last backpacking trip by ourselves. We often allotted four or five days for one of these adventures, knowing it would often be shorter due to one of our rules. The rule was, "Always quit while you're having fun." So we were prepared for about four days. I carried thirty-two pounds and she had twenty-three, much less than we had taken for half the time and more than twice the people twenty years before. And we had plenty. We had learned a few things in twenty years on the trails about what we really needed. And we had also learned that some of the resources we needed were right there in the woods; we didn't need to haul everything on our backs. That left a great deal more room to enjoy life and each other, and to hear the whispers of God's still, small voice through the trees and in the streams.

THE VALLEYS

We had to leave encumbrances behind in the valley. You can't take a car into the wilderness. And there aren't plugs for electric appliances. We had to make a choice between the comforts of car camping and the solitude, freedom, spiritual exhilaration, and intimacy with God we could have without the stuff in the car or a full hookup.

Now for most activities in modern life, a car is considered a necessity. We enjoy having motorized transportation; in fact we name our vehicles. The one we have now is "Georgie Girl." But some urban dwellers, folks in parts of Europe, backpackers, and the Amish would question whether a car is really a necessity. In fact I don't remember reading about what kind of car Jesus had, though he did ride a burro once. I sometimes feel that when it comes to meeting our true needs, less is more.

This is a valley in which we fear insufficiency, that our needs won't be supplied. This fear is built around two false assumptions: first, that we need what we want and, second, that the world can teach us what we should want. *Wants equal needs. Culture teaches needs*. Let's explore these further.

Wants Equal Needs

One of the first questions I ask married couples in counseling is, "What do you *want* for your marriage?" Then, as the timing seems right, I ask the underlying question: "What do you *need* in your marriage?" Occasionally a couple will look at me sort of quizzically, as if those are two forms of the same question. But if the counseling process is effective, they come to understand that what they *want* and what they *need* are often two very different things.

The biblical terms for wanting or desiring are much richer than our English equivalents. The term often translated "lust" *(epithumia)* has to do with intense, passionate desire and is sometimes portrayed in a negative light, but Jesus uses that term when He says, "I have eagerly desired to eat this Passover with you before I suffer" (Luke 22:15). So the good or bad quality of that intense, passionate desire depends on the object that is wanted. Another term, often translated in verb form as "to want," also has to do with desire; Jesus uses this term when he asks the lame man at the pool, "Do you want to get well?" (John 5: 6). A third term for desire, choice, or wants has to do with a choice between alternatives rather than an emotional desire; this term is used by Pilate when he asks the crowd, just before the crucifixion, if they choose for him to release Jesus or Barabbas (see John 18:39–40).

When I ask a couple what they want and then what they need, I have two of these biblical concepts in mind. On the one hand, what would you like to do with this marriage? Do you want to stay together and grow old in the unity you can achieve? On the other hand, what, in light of your legacy, do you *need*? Wants have to do with what you desire; needs have to do with what your life is intended to look like, what you are on this earth for, what will give you the most satisfaction with your life a hundred years from now.

One of the errors most of us make is to assume that we need whatever we want. We want to have a higher income, a bigger house, more sex with our spouse, a better golf score, a faster car, and the latest smartphone and other electronic gadget. And if we want it, we must need it. And if we need it as much as we want it, then surely our prayers will be answered that God will give it!

Then we wonder why our needs outlast our resources. It doesn't matter if we're talking about marital, medical, vocational, parenting, recreational, or any of the other resources we want. If we equate our wants and our needs, we will not have enough. We will run out of the resources God provides. If we allow God to bless us with a return to what we *need* rather than what we *want*, we can begin to leave the valley and step out onto the path toward the heavenly places where our needs are abundantly supplied.

Culture Teaches Needs

It is not easy to leave this valley, though, partly because the culture we live in is so very loudly and skillfully telling us what we should want. How many folks have you heard say that regardless of the quality of the football, the Super Bowl is so worth watching because of the ads? Goodness, I have said that myself. We just love to have somebody tell us what chips, what beer, what car, what phone, what yogurt, what cereal, what computer, and what soft drink you have got to have if you're going to have a good life. There's something in me that recoils when I hear that this phone, book, mattress, suit, or car is the one I've "got to have." No, as a matter of fact, I don't "got to have it."

Counselors of all kinds hear couples say over and over, year after year, "We just want things to be like they were when we were first married." Who taught us that we need or deserve for things to be just as good (in just the same way) when we're seventy as they were when we were thirty?

The valley of the shadow of the death of our resources is filled with frustrated wants we interpret as needs because our culture—the biblical term is "the world"—fills us with false needs. Let's use a simple example of what this does to us. Let's say my wife and I need $40 worth of groceries to last us a week. But when Calder goes to the store she's hungry. And not only that, we watched the Super Bowl just the day before. We may not get the chips and beer they advertised, but we both love cheese and crackers. Oh, and doesn't God promise us chocolate, both ice cream and cookies? And it's starting to warm up, so let's have steak on the grill. (Remember the couple having so much fun grilling in the ad?) And steel cut oats are mighty healthy, but the box of cereal is so much easier; Oh, and that good brand is supposed to have all the vitamins we need. And I'm about to run out of lipstick, and that lady on…—so, let's get some more lipstick. And before I go home, well, I could wash the car at home, but the car wash is quicker and then I wouldn't even think about a new car. Get the point? A $40 grocery bill can wind up being $240—or more!—if we allow our culture to tell us what we need. And then we wonder what happened to the provision we thought God promised.

THE PATHS

If someone told you they could assure you that you would have all you need throughout your life, would you be interested? God promises just that: "And my God will meet all your needs according to the riches of his glory in Christ Jesus" (Phil. 4:19). The context of that verse is the Philippians' gifts to support Paul's ministry and the fact that there were limited resources for anyone living in the first century. There were no government bailouts for the Christians at Philippi. Yet God said through Paul that the Philippian Christians would not be deprived due to their sacrificial giving. There were no bailouts for the people called Methodist during the eighteenth century. Yet John Wesley made it clear that part of the responsibility of the church of God's people is to collect funds from those who are amply supplied and to care for widows, orphans, and others who are in need.[1] Both Paul and Wesley and other leaders of the church know that God supplies our needs. But that supply depends on adherence to two simple principles: accurately *defining the need* and *identifying the resources* that God provides.

Defining the Need

The definition of "just what I need" is like some cairns on a climb: stones are strewn about, barely marking the outline of a cairn, and the trail is difficult to discern. It is easier above timberline, where map and compass can show the way, but trail definition is much more difficult in a wooded area. We have often used not only cairns, map, and compass but also signs (cairns without stones, if you will), such as breaks in the trees, grass that seems more compressed, rocks that have been turned over by hikers' boots, the direction of the wind, the direction of game trails, and sometimes just pure intuition. The trail, like our needs, is not clearly defined.

There have been many books written about the *definition of our needs*: Maslow's hierarchy of needs comes to mind, of course,[2] and Harley's wonderful book *His Needs, Her Needs*.[3] Richard Foster's books on Christian simplicity and discipline offer some helpful insight into our needs.[4] John and Stasi Eldredge in both *Wild at Heart* [5]and the companion volume *Captivating*[6] have written effectively and in a way I personally identify with concerning gender-specific needs. The list goes on and becomes in many ways quite complex.

A simple definition of our needs would help us know what to expect from God's resources. There are two elements that can help us in the definition of our needs: the strength and weaknesses we bring to the point of need.

Several years ago my family and I were planning on a fairly long backpacking trip into the Weminuche Wilderness north of Durango, Colorado. We were packed, in pretty good shape, and had adequate knowledge of the area and its challenges from map study and one previous backpacking trip. We took the train north to Elk Park, disembarked, and began our adventure. We hiked in about five miles and set up camp with a wonderful view of Vestal Peak, Wham Ridge, and other hills of the western end of that wilderness. We had planned to go up and over Hunchback Pass, down Vallecito Creek Valley, then up and over Columbine Pass into the beautiful Chicago Basin, then out to the train pickup about five or six days later. It would have been an exhilarating trip, one our family would never forget, the stories of which would be passed down for generations. We felt we needed that trip.

But *defining the needs* depends on the strengths and weaknesses we bring to the point of need. We had each had bouts of altitude sickness before; usually the one of us in the best physical condition had the worst altitude difficulties—dizziness, loss of appetite, lack of thirst, headache, and general malaise. Well, this time I developed the worst altitude sickness I ever had on a backpacking trip. The balance of my strengths and weaknesses redefined our needs.

We left, went to another wilderness area at a lower altitude, and had a wonderful time. We had to alter the *definition of our needs* according to our strengths and weaknesses.

There was a couple once who had a beautiful and very fulfilling marriage, a quite lively daughter they had adopted, and an extraordinarily friendly German shepherd who was very protective of their daughter. This couple had it all: intimacy, good communication, effective coping with medical needs, a powerful love for God, plenty of money from his work as an engineer, and an active church life. They even had a pretty positive relationship with all the in-laws! But there was one element of marriage they did not have, an element that most people would say is one of the primary needs in all marriage. They had no sexual relationship in any traditional sense at all, except affectionate touching. She was paraplegic. She had been through a terrible car wreck soon after they were married and had no feeling below her waist. But they had the resilience and willingness to alter the *definition of their needs* according to their unique strengths and weaknesses. They had as a result a marriage that was rich far beyond many others who had a "normal" supply of their needs.

Our needs are not the same. Our strengths and weaknesses are not the same. God does not supply our needs by a supernatural conveyor belt that doles out the same things to all of us. One of the problems with our understanding of God's enriching our lives well beyond all we could ask or think (see 1 Corinthians 2:9) is that God loves and provides for us as individuals. Some of us would be quite uncomfortable backpacking and sleeping on the ground. Others would be uncomfortable attending the opera. Some don't know or care about research design. Some don't eat asparagus under any hunger situation. I have even heard that there are those unfortunates who don't think they need coffee! God meets our needs according not only to his riches in glory but according to the unique strengths and weaknesses we bring to the point of need.

One other note: God sometimes alters the *definition of our needs* by what he provides. He did that with me a while back when he called me to a third career at seventy years old. I certainly didn't think I needed another career in ministry. Yes, I had been thinking about this book for a long time. But surely I needed to retire. God knew better. He changed my understanding of what I needed by what he provided.

Identifying the Resources

Who would have thought that a couple of fish and five loaves of bread could feed five thousand men? That event is very important to each of the biblical writers (see Matthew 14:13–21; Mark 6:32–44; Luke 9:10–17; John 6:1–13). It is also very important to our building the cairn of God's resources to supply our needs. We miss the point of this event if we focus on the psychological or physiological means of Jesus' feeding the crowd. He *identified the resources* and made those resources work to meet the need at hand.

Military and law enforcement servants to our country and communities are to be admired, respected, and can teach us some things about life in Christ. Effective military and law enforcement service requires an ability to adapt to the resources that are available in any given situation. Conventional weapons, medical tools, food, shelter, or other necessities are not always readily available. I have tremendous admiration for the survivalist mentality that can identify resources where there seem to be none. Each of us has the opportunity at some point in our lives to learn to exercise some ingenuity identifying the resources that God has placed before us to meet our needs.

I became depressed after my left artificial hip was surgically revised in 1998. I was actually sort of surprised by that turn of events. I'm a Christian, a counselor, and would have thought I'd know how to prevent depression. I later found out that my potassium and sodium were out of whack, but I didn't know that as I lay there feeling sad. I just knew I needed for something to happen to lift that cloud above my head. I prayed, listened, talked to my wife and boys, and tried to find an empathetic ear that would help somewhere.

Then I made a choice. I would do something to help with whatever was at hand. Resources were limited, but then the Holy Spirit reminded me that I still had my mind and my rather impaired and shackled body. I said, "OK, Lord, let's start getting ready for me to climb a fourteen thousand foot peak within twelve months." And I began to work my feet back and forth, exercising my calves. That exercise began the process that ended with me and my wife summiting Mount Princeton nine months later, on Sept. 17, 1999. (There's more detail in Appendix A). God used the resources at hand to meet my needs.

THE HEAVENLY PLACES

Healthy Christian people don't just get by; we thrive. If we are willing to let God *define our needs* and *identify the resources* he can use to meet those needs, we become rich folks. Paul said, "You know the grace of our Lord Jesus Christ, that though he was rich, yet for your sake he became poor, so that you through his poverty might become rich" (2 Cor. 8:9). He was not just talking about money. He was talking about our becoming rich with the life of Jesus Christ flowing within us and through us as we walk around the heavenly places in the resource fullness of God himself. If we allow ourselves to be "filled with all the fullness of God" (Eph. 3:19, NKJV), we can experience the cup of our lives *overflowing with grace* and filled with *undisappointed hope.*

Overflow of Grace

"My cup overflows…" says the psalmist (Ps. 23:5). It is one of the great ironies of life in Christ: if we hunger and thirst for and eat and drink deeply from the gifts of God's grace, if we ask with Jabez that God would bless us indeed and enhance our lives (see 1 Chronicles 4:10), we can find that our lives become a source of grace and blessing to those around us. If we let God love us, we find that we love ourselves, others, God, and life itself. If we let God meet our needs, we become amply supplied to meet the needs of others.

Students and occasionally church members who have consulted with me about a position in the helping services or professions have wondered about burning out. It is especially true of mothers, and most especially mothers who have a career outside the home, that they wonder, "Will I have enough? Will I have enough energy for my children if I take this Sunday school class or this committee assignment, or help organize this women's conference?" Let me say I am the first to encourage restraint in overextension. We live in a hyperactive society and I don't for a minute want to add to the frenetic energy of the twenty-first century. But the dynamic relationship of giving and receiving grace is such that our needs are met in the process of giving—if our giving is an *overflow of grace.*

It is not only students and volunteers who need to be advised that our own cup must be filled as the basis for service. I know personally how easy it is for a minister to substitute sermon preparation for devotional nurture. I also know how easy it can be for a writer to focus on the needs of potential readers and to neglect exercise or taking your wife to dinner and a movie. And how many counselors have neglected their own psychological needs in the process of helping others. And, doctors, how many of you have I seen who will rise up early, stay up late, and join every medical committee in town to help their patients while their own health suffers? God wants to supply our needs in such a way that all our service and work for him are an overflow of the grace with which he has first filled our own cup, after which he reaches through us into the needs of others.

Undisappointed Hope

The goal of the previous chapters has been freedom from false hopes that would leave us disappointed in life and angry at God, a description of cairns that build good hope, and authentic pictures of life in the heavenly places of hope. We have explored our values and have examined the resources that God provides for our lives. We have seen that when God is meeting our needs, "hope does not disappoint, because the love of God has been poured out in our hearts by the Holy Spirit who was given to us" (Rom. 5:5). It is important on the one hand not to minimize or criticize the hopes of any readers from the Christian community. It is also important that we take caution to avoid setting God up for failure. If we put words in God's mouth that he has not spoken, we run the risk of taking God's name in vain. We do not need to put words in God's mouth, however; for the promise of his Word is nothing short of the fullness of his riches in glory in the heavenly places in Christ. That is our hope. And it is enough.

THE QUESTIONS AND SCRIPTURES

1. What disappointed hopes have you experienced? How did that disappointment affect you? How did you try to resolve that problem?
2. What need has frustrated you? How might God meet that need? What would happen if you tried for one week to let God define that need and identify resources that he makes available to meet that need?
3. What are you afraid you might lose if you let God meet your needs? What might you gain instead of the thing you fear losing?
4. Do you have needs that may be wants rather than needs? Is there a real need underlying your wants? What is that need and how might God want to meet that need?
5. Who would really do the best job at meeting your needs?
6. What would God want you to do to take care of yourself in meeting your needs? What choices might God want to use to love you (for example, exercise, getting to bed earlier, taking a day off each week, spending time every week with your spouse or best friend, etc.)?
7. If your life were filled with the resources God provides, who in your life would benefit most besides you?
8. Scripture for further reflection: 1 Kings 17:1–19:18; Ps. 23, 118; Matt. 6:25–34; John 6:1–13; 2 Cor. 8:1–15; Phil. 4:10–19.

CHAPTER 13
PLEASURE: HOW CAN I ENJOY LIFE?

The lay leader of the Melvin United Methodist Church was a wise man. He could express in simple, south Alabama language the wisdom of scholars and the insights of erudite pundits. One of his most frequent sayings was, "Most people do what they want to do; so if they're going to do the right thing, they've got to want to do the right thing." One of his illustrations concerned giving money to the church. He would often say that it took three generations to teach someone to become a real giver because it took that long for folks to learn that giving is a pleasure.

Popular psychology refers to one of the driving forces in life as "the pleasure principle." That phrase has been transferred from Freudian psychology into music, fashion, and commercial marketing as one of the goals of a good life. But the money, the energy, the frenetic acquisition of more and more stuff, and the almost desperate grasping for pleasure in our culture make me ask the question: Are we having fun yet?

Can we enjoy life? What is the place of pleasure in Christian life? Or is pleasure contrary to life in Christ?

Jesus portrayed the need for an enjoyable or pleasurable life in his parables and throughout his life and saving work. His teaching on prayer in Luke 11, for example, shows clearly that God wants to give good gifts to his children. He says, with the humor characteristic of many of his parables, that if a child asks a father for a fish or an egg, he would not be given a snake or a scorpion. Jesus, "though he was rich, yet for your sake he became poor, so that you through his poverty might become rich" (2 Cor. 8:9). He befriends and cares for us in a way that we may "have life, and have it to the full" (John 10:10). Christians may be called to leave family and possessions, but they can be sure that they will, in this life, receive it all back, with interest (see Mark 10:28–31).

The Greek term that is most often translated "blessed" can also be translated "happy" (see, for example, Matthew 5:3–11); the blessed life we are given in Christ is a happy, pleasurable life. Another Greek term used by Augustine of Hippo and other church fathers to describe the Christian life is best translated as "well-being" as well as "happy." Augustine is a good starting point for any discussion of pleasure as a worthwhile goal of Christian life. For the pleasure Augustine found in Christ was far different than the pleasure he achieved cavorting with the wild and wanton entertainments afforded by Carthaginian culture. He indicated at one point that he wanted to accept Christ, but only after he had enjoyed the sinful pleasures of Carthage a bit longer. Augustine wandered in the valley of unsatisfied, restless life until he came to rest and the enjoyment of Christ.[1]

Pleasure is not contrary to life in Christ; it is part of life in Christ. John Piper develops this so very well in his book *Desiring God;* our very purpose as God's people is to glorify God by enjoying him, by enjoying the life he gives.[2] But we've got to leave the dark valley of dysfunctional, sinful pleasure in order to enjoy the "pleasures at (God's) right hand" (Ps. 16:11).

THE VALLEYS

There are two sources of pleasure that leave us frustrated, unsatisfied, and deficient in the joy we seek: *narcissism* and *flesh.* We can pursue pleasure in Christ or apart from Christ, in healthy ways or unhealthy ways. The terms *flesh* and *narcissism* reflect two different perspectives, one biblical and one psychological, on the same phenomenon: dysfunctional, self-contained attempts to achieve pleasure.

Narcissism

The person with this personality disorder may appear to be boastful, arrogant, and selfish, but usually those appearances hide a sense of shame, worthlessness, and low self-esteem. A *narcissistic* person, as we mentioned briefly earlier, will often seek to gather the world around him or herself, seeking pleasure at the expense of and sometimes in abusive manipulation of others. This person may be very successful, ambitious, and impressive to others. In fact our culture often rewards *narcissism* with awards and accolades.

There are three dominant characteristics of *narcissism:* entitlement, superiority, and grandiosity. The narcissist considers that the world owes him or her a pleasurable existence, and that those pleasures can be defined in whatever way he or she wishes. It is easy for narcissists to believe that God has been unfair if something does not happen their way on their time-frame. Sometimes people who are angry at God, spouse, or life suffer from this underlying disorder. God healed Job of a narcissistic demand for God's answers through his sufferings. I know personally that deliverance from the painful valley of narcissism is important for lasting sobriety.

Narcissism, like life in the *flesh*, may look glamorous and wealthy. The grandiosity of *narcissism* makes a big splash and is full of impressive stuff. But this valley is actually quite devoid of satisfaction.

Flesh

Few words in the Bible are as misunderstood as the term *flesh*. The word does not just refer to a good steak or a person's body, although sometimes it does, as when Jesus says after the resurrection, "A ghost does not have flesh and bones, as you see I have" (Luke 24:39). But when Paul draws a contrast between life in the Spirit and life in the *flesh*, he is using the term to represent humankind apart from and in enmity with God (see Romans 7–8).

The pleasures of the flesh are not just bodily pleasures, but any pleasures that are sought, nurtured, and experienced outside of a relationship with God. Sexual immorality and gluttony, for example, fail to bring real pleasure because those behaviors are at enmity with God. Sexual immorality and gluttony do not achieve pleasure; they destroy pleasure. They are not just sinful because they are bad; they are bad because they, like all narcissistic and fleshly attempts to achieve pleasure, simply do not work. The pleasures of the flesh and the pleasure-seeking of narcissism are, in the end, different streams flowing into the same river of a failed solution to our need for pleasure.

Abstinence from flesh or narcissism is not enough to take us out of this valley of frustrated pleasure. I struggled for several years during the seventies to achieve sobriety through abstinence alone. I asked a counselor in south Alabama what I needed in order to be consistently sober and expected him to say that I needed to take the third step, or to do a real good fourth step, or some other aspect of the Alcoholics Anonymous program. He said, instead, "You need eventually to find something you enjoy more than you did drinking." Abstinence alone was not enough. I needed to find pleasure in Christ.

If we seek only abstinence from pleasure of the flesh or of a narcissistic lifestyle, we will leave ourselves at risk of a return to the only pleasures we have known. If we do not allow God to meet our needs for pleasure in Christ, we are often vulnerable to entrapment in the valley of pleasure apart from Christ. Some of the dramatic downfalls of prominent ministers demonstrate this vulnerability. If we do not allow ourselves to enjoy life in the Spirit, we are susceptible to returning to our former enjoyments of the flesh. If we do not allow God to meet our pleasure needs in ways that are psychologically healthy, we tend to become narcissistic. Jesus showed this in his parable of a house that is left clean of evil but empty; it is then vulnerable to reoccupation by a worse evil (see Matthew 12:43–45). The fullness of God, the pleasures at his right hand (see Psalm 16:11), can protect us against that vulnerability.

THE PATHS

Let's get out of that valley! The valley of frustrated, dissatisfied pleasure, like many valleys in *Climbing Home*, can leave us feeling suffocated. It's time to get positive about this pleasure business. The cairns that indicate the path forward are the *pleasure of God*, the *pleasure of others,* and combining *delayed gratification* with *undelayed gratitude*.

Pleasure of God

Whatever pleases God will please us. The Bible is full of passages about our blessing God and the result in our own blessing:

> Bless the Lord, O my soul,
>   And all that is within me,

Bless his holy name.
Bless the Lord, O my soul,
And forget not all his benefits—
…who satisfies you with good
So that your youth is renewed like the eagle's. (Ps. 103:1–2, 5, ESV)

And from Ephesians: "Blessed be the God and Father of our Lord Jesus Christ, who has blessed us with every spiritual blessing in the heavenly places in Christ" (Eph. 1:3, NKJV).

These passages that correlate our pleasure and the pleasure of God call to mind the godliness we discussed at the beginning of the book. It may be a bit counterintuitive to our messed-up human natures, but pleasing God, like godliness, brings us just what we need: the pleasure and truthful perception that is so elusive to us.

Let's use some specific examples of how this might work. Two of the areas that come to most of our minds where pleasure is concerned are eating and sexual activity. Eating in a responsible, healthy manner might not look, at first sight, like a pleasurable thing. But compare the long-term effects of healthy eating with the habitual ingestion of unhealthy junk food, which neither pleases God nor keeps us healthy and happy. Which is really pleasurable over the course of a lifetime?

Our sexual fulfillment in Christ can be indescribably pleasurable when it takes place in the context of lifelong marital fidelity. It wouldn't appear in a popular movie, but there are few sexual experiences that can bring more pleasure than my wife and I know when she takes my arm walking into a restaurant. That's fulfilling because it rests on a foundation of many years of growing love expressed through diverse kinds of intimacy. It pleases God. And it pleases us.

The experience of sexual pleasure in Christ is such an important and large subject that it requires whole books to explore, not just part of a chapter. There are a number of books written from an evangelical standpoint that are very helpful in this area, including *The Gift of Sex* by Clifford and Joyce Penner[3] and *Authentic Human Sexuality* by Judith and Jack Balswick.[4]

Two things need to be said in the context of *Climbing Home:* first, the culture we live in does not teach realistic sexual fulfillment. And second, it is God's will that his people experience the blessing of sexual fulfillment. God does not want us to get filled with the Spirit and turn off our sexuality any more than he wants us to turn off the pleasure of a sunset or the enjoyment of the heavenly taste of my wife's bread. What he does want and will teach us is responsibility and gratitude. Those please him.

Whatever pleases God will please us; this principle can be applied to our enjoyment of life as a whole.

Think for a moment about the Ten Commandments. Several years ago I did three series of sermons in three different churches focused on God's positive invitation to a productive, pleasurable life that underlies each of the commandments. The commandment not to steal, for example, rests on God's invitation to the joy of work well done. The commandment not to covet rests on God's invitation to enjoy the pleasures and gifts that are uniquely ours rather than fretting about something he has given someone else. The commandment to keep the Sabbath day is one that both physicians and psychotherapists would agree we need in our overworked society. And it's right there in the Bible that it's not only OK to rest and play, it pleases God. Whatever pleases God can bring us pleasure.

Pleasing Others

Do you begin to see the ironic paradox in pleasure? Whatever pleases God pleases us, and whatever pleases those we love and care about also pleases us. This is certainly counterintuitive, though, isn't it? Any parent knows that sharing is something that must be learned, and sometimes those lessons don't come easy. Remember the lay leader at the beginning of this chapter? I often wondered why he would have said it takes three generations to create a truly giving person. Now I understand that it takes time to learn that there is pleasure in giving.

There is an intervention that was developed in one area of marital therapy that I have often used in helping couples grow in their love and marital satisfaction. It's called the odd/even day assignment. Let's say a couple is having difficulty sharing housework. Perhaps the wife not only does the cooking and laundry but also does the grass, rakes the leaves, changes the oil in the car, washes the windows, and cleans the bathrooms. The husband may feel that he works all day at the office or the oilfield or wherever his job may be, so when he gets home it's time for TV and something cold to drink. He may take out the garbage and take the kids to school, but that's about it concerning sharing domestic tasks. It's amazing what can happen if every other day the wife goes with him to his job and he does all the housework, then they switch (maybe on a Saturday) and the wife watches TV and the husband does all the housework. They often decide pretty quickly that sharing isn't so bad after all. They can begin to learn that giving is pleasure.

My wife worked nights as a nurse for several years after my family and I moved to west Texas. It worked out pretty well with our boys' school schedule; she would wake from her day's sleep about the time they got home from school. I was at school myself from about 9:00 AM to 9:00 PM, which meant that the boys and I had a great time with our breakfast ritual. The other part of our arrangement was that during the summer I would do all the childcare. The first two weeks of each summer were like a vacation: pool, playing hide-and-go-seek, all sorts of fun. But of course by August, I was ready for school to start!

Another part of our arrangement was that as long as my wife was working nights, she would never wash a dish, vacuum a floor, straighten a room, or take out the garbage. We adopted a philosophy of work that was sort of like that of the agricultural world. We didn't have man's work, woman's work, and children playing; there was Thomas family work. And we loved it. We took pride and found pleasure in sharing the Thomas family jobs, be they writing a paper, doing the dishes, nursing the patients, or doing the homework. Then when Friday night came, there was no work, no study, no nursing even. For six years, Friday night and Saturday morning were Sabbath time. My goodness, did we ever have fun. The shared work that led to the play contributed to our pleasure.

Delayed Gratification, Undelayed Gratitude

Delayed gratification is not fun and seems, at first glance, inconsistent with pleasure.[5] I remember as a child being irritated that I had to wait until third grade to have paper with thin lines and skinny pencils; until then it was that rough, unlined paper and the fat pencils. Then I had to wait to drive a car; I cared about my mother but I was glad she had the back trouble that kept her from reaching the pedals on our old 1955 Plymouth; her medical condition meant I got to drive her to the chiropractor when I was eleven! Then I had to wait for college, then for other good things of life. Delayed gratification, indeed! I didn't find it very gratifying at all.

There are three things that can make delayed gratification a part of our experience of a pleasurable, enjoyable life. The first of these is the pleasure of the moment. It is likely that in a society that raises hurried children, as David Elkind powerfully points out in his book *The Hurried Child,* that we are teaching pleasure as something that is always in the future; our culture doesn't emphasize parenting for responsible pleasure with what we have, here and now.[6] Parental presence in play can help a child know the pleasure of the toys, games, and other means of pleasure that are available in the present moment. This is something that I often challenge clients, students, and church members to do: Stop and look around at the things, people, songs, events, jobs, or acts of kindness and love that can make this day pleasurable. We don't have to wait for all gratification, just the gratification that is still in the future.

A second factor in accepting and even enjoying life in delayed gratification is memory. I personally am quite excited to move on to the next phase of my life and find out what heaven is like. Now, don't get me wrong, my wife and I are enjoying life more now than we ever have, albeit with a bit less energy, vim, and vigor than twenty years ago. But one of the reasons we are enjoying the delay of heaven's gate is that we are having so much fun with memory. Just this morning I began to sing, "There's a land that is fairer than day, and I know I shall see it someday; dyaw lee dyaw law dee law dyaw lee dyaw. . . ." Then I said, "Calder, we need to watch that show again soon." She knew immediately I was referring to the movie with Sally Field and Danny Glover, *Places in the Heart.*[7] Memory brings us pleasure while we wait for the gratification that will come for us soon enough in heaven.

The third element of pleasure through delayed gratification is undelayed gratitude. This is closely related to finding pleasure in the moment. The most beautiful human beings I have known have been those who express gratitude on a daily basis for the gifts of God that are all around us, filling each day with pleasure.

One of our next door neighbors in Melvin, Alabama was a considerable bit older than I when I pastored her church. She lived a modest but comfortable life, though some would say she lived far below her means. Perhaps she did live more simply than she had to, considering her resources. But I'll never forget one day walking over to her house to visit her and her husband. She was singing as I walked up to the open door of the house, "There's within my heart a melody, Jesus whispers sweet and low; fear not I am with you, peace be still, in all of life's ebb and flow; Jesus, Jesus, Jesus. . . ." I listened a moment, then knocked, and was greeted by, "Well, hello, preacher; isn't this a fine day for you to come visiting, though!" She knew the pleasure of gratitude that is undelayed and constant in season and out of season. She knew how to do pleasure.

THE HEAVENLY PLACES

Pleasure in Christ looks like the joy of the Lord, and the joy of the Lord has at least two specific dimensions: *strength* and *glory*.

Strength

"The joy of the Lord is your strength" (Neh. 8:10). A part of that strength is the ability to live within one's means. That is not only a financial concept. It also applies, in my case, to enjoying life when mountain-climbing days are over but life is very much ongoing. There are ads, about which I will not be too specific, which are oriented around the desire of male people to have the same kind of strength in certain areas that they had when they were twenty or thirty. Now that's just fine, and maybe those ads represent an intervention that would be pleasing to God and to others, like wives. But there is a different kind of strength that is part of the joy of the Lord: the strength to enjoy your life and ability where they are. I defy any man of any age to show me anything more pleasurable than reaching over to hold my wife's hand in church. That's strong pleasure, rooted in the joy of the Lord.

Glory

The glory of God is the beauty, the power, the good, and the wonderful qualities of God. It's the pastel colors of early morning sunrise, the light in a child's eyes, the twinkle in the eyes of an old couple walking through the park, the first cry of a baby, the whisper of the Spirit during a hymn, and the feel of a pillow after a good day's work. The glory of God is the greatness of God spread across the tapestry of our lives, woven into life's texture, warming us on a cold winter's night. The glory of God is the appearance of Jesus in the midst of our infirmities, as Charles Wesley put it:

> Hear him, ye deaf; his praise, ye dumb,
>   Your loosened tongues employ;
> Ye blind behold your Savior come,
>   And leap ye lame for joy.

The glory of God is the life of God around us, within us, and through us pouring grace into the hearts of those we love. The glory of God is the foundation, the essence, and the experience of pleasure. That glory of God is, above all, what pleasure looks like in the heavenly places in Jesus Christ.

THE QUESTIONS AND SCRIPTURES

1. What are the five greatest sources of pleasure for you? How long do those pleasures last? Are those pleasures followed by more pleasure—or sorrow?
2. How have you been taught to avoid pleasure, or that pleasure is bad? What does the Bible say about such lessons (see

for example Psalm 37; Habakkuk. 3:17–19; John 10:10; 1 John 1)?

3. What gives God the greatest pleasure about your life? What is the relation between God's pleasure about your life and your pleasure?
4. What in your life gives others pleasure?
5. What five things would bring more pleasure to both you and God? What will you do this week to implement one of those things?
6. Try naming something every day for a month for which you are grateful. How does that affect the level of pleasure in your life?
7. Today, do something for no good reason except that you want to, for the person you love most in your life. Who gained the most pleasure from what you did?
8. Scripture for further reflection: Ps. 16, 103; Matt. 5:3–11; Rom. 7, 8; Phil. 4:4–19.

CHAPTER 14

PAIN: HOW CAN I ENDURE?

Your life is, at times, painful. Of course, I have not met most of you. But, then, I *have* met you. I have met you in church members, students, counseling clients, therapists I have supervised, family, and friends. I have heard your pain, have shared your struggles, and have seen your lives rise from the ashes of your fiery afflictions. And I hope, just a little, to reflect in this chapter what you have taught me about the life God can bring out of pain.

Your lives are diverse. You are teachers, farmers, mothers, fathers, accountants, oilfield workers, insurance salespeople, store clerks, preachers, construction folks, realtors, and counselors. You are young and old, wealthy and poor, pretty and athletic, overweight and medically challenged, very Christian and struggling with spirituality. Some are patriotic, some are from the Anglo-Saxon South, some are Mexican-American, and some are African-American. Some of you are Catholic, some Methodist, some Baptist, and many of you attend either non-denominational churches or no church at all.

You have experienced a wide variety of answers to the problem of pain. You have read books, heard sermons, been treated by doctors, talked to counselors, and visited with trusted family and friends to get answers. And some of you have answered pain by hiding it. You have kept your pain to yourselves, have been embarrassed to show the pain you feel. Remember the time you fell on the playground or had your feelings hurt by your best friend or had to walk from a field in defeat? Remember how you tried, sometimes in vain, to prevent anyone from seeing your tears or your quivering lower lip? Remember how you got mad rather than show the pain you felt?

Others of you have fought the sources of pain. You have built strong defenses against the enemies of your well-being and that of your loved ones. You have become warriors, not only protecting yourself and your family from pain but also protecting your neighborhood, your country, and perhaps your church. You have become an expert at weeding out and attacking evil in every form.

Some of you have known the pain of loss, others the pain of never finding. Some have known the excruciating pain of losing a child; others have known the very different but very difficult pain of infertility. Some of you have known the pain of job loss; you may also have known the prolonged agony of looking for but not finding a job. Some of you have courageously kept on and on at a job you don't like, detest even, but you've kept on working to provide for those you love. Some of you have known the pain of addiction, others have suffered patiently with boredom.

You have taught me about pain, and I have listened. You have asked your question of pain in my counseling office, in church foyers, in hospitals, in funeral homes, on front porches as I visited, and after class as we talked over a lesson then later addressed your real question.

You have asked, "How can I endure?" And as I have been privileged to listen to how you and God answered your own question, you have taught me. And I hope to recreate an outline of what you and I together have heard and learned. You have taught me that, in Christ, pain is not so much a problem as it is the constricting of the womb of God out of which we are born into newness of life.

THE VALLEYS

You have not only taught me the life that can emerge from pain; you have also shown me the valley that holds us away from the path toward resurrection. That valley has two streams that are as familiar as they are difficult to leave behind: *flight* and *fight*.

Each of these is ambiguous, however, and cannot be seen only as a failed solution to the problem of pain. There is a healthy and biblical place for *flight*. "God is our refuge and strength…" (Ps. 46:1). "You are my hiding place…" (Ps. 32:7). The commandment to keep the Sabbath day is God's invitation for us to take flight from the world of work once a week. And Jesus invited the disciples, when they needed a break, "Come with me by yourselves to a quiet place and get some rest" (Mark 6:31).

There is also a healthy and biblical place for fighting the forces of evil and other destruction of our lives. The armor of God (Eph. 6:10–17) is designed to protect and equip the warrior of God "against powers, against the rulers of the darkness of this age, against spiritual hosts of wickedness in the heavenly places" (Eph. 6:12, NKJV).

There is a part of the gospel that I would challenge us to consider, however. Those who *fight* against crime, fire, and the enemies of our values have taught me this principle. The *fight* against evil in all of its forms can take over a person's life in such a way that there's not much room left for family, friends, or growth in Christ. The Good News is that Jesus Christ has overcome the world (see John 16:33). He has said of the final destruction of evil and pain and death "It is finished" (John 19:30).

Yes we can and should enjoy the flight from pain that is provided by a good vacation; we can and should continue to fight the evils of our society or of medical or psychological pathology. And no, we are not to live with our heads in the clouds of some heavenly places in such a way that we're no earthly good. But because Jesus Christ has triumphed over the defining power of pain to tell us who we are, because in him the accuser is thrown down and the King of Kings and Lord of Lords sits on the throne, because Jesus has accomplished the salvation of his people, pain does not need to define us any longer. It can be the canal through which we pass to new experiences of joy and gladness and hope, even as we remain in the midst of pain. We do not need to be obsessively defined by the fight with an enemy who is defeated, nor spend all our lives taking flight from pain that cannot snatch us from the hand of our Savior.

Oscar Cullman, in his classic book, *Christ and Time,* has provided one of the most helpful discussions of the tension between what God has already done in Christ and what is yet to be done at his second coming.[1] All too obviously, pain and evil are still in this world. And yet it is also true that the victory over sin and death and pain are guaranteed in the cross and resurrection of Jesus. Cullman compares the "already" and "not yet" of our life in Christ to the difference between D-day and V-day in World War II. The victory of America and her allies against Hitler was virtually assured at D-day, but there were still battles to be fought before

V-Day. The same is true for those who would seek to live healthy lives in Christ. Our victory is sure in such a way that pain, though all too real and powerful, does not need to define us.

Our flight and fight responses to pain keep us down in a valley of failure only when we live as if the battle with pain belongs entirely to us. The path forward out of the valley depends on our recognition that ultimately "the battle is not yours, but God's" (2 Chron. 20:15).

Flight

When I was a little boy I had two hiding places in the backyard. One was the open center of a group of bushes in the back corner of the yard. Only very special friends were allowed to know where it was, and my parents could never know (I thought, anyhow) the location of my special refuge. The other place was high up in a mulberry tree; I felt like I could see the whole world from those heights, but the world could not see me. There wasn't anything wrong with having my special places. But when I took *flight* from others when life was painful, I was beginning a pattern that would plague me for much of my life. Later forms of my flight from reality became not only addictive but intensified the pain I sought to escape.

One problem with flight is that it doesn't always seem negative. In fact, many of the hiding places of our world are good. Work, for example, is a good thing. But when work becomes a hiding place from marriage and family, and even from God, work can turn into a prison. Remember Jesus' warning about tearing down barns to build bigger barns (Luke 12:18)? That can apply to Christian "barns" as well as agricultural enterprise.

Some flight patterns have affected our society as a whole. It is truly amazing what an escapist society we have become. People walk into water fountains while texting, gamers in front of a little screen lose the ability to play with a real group of people, and our society seems to have lost the ability to do pleasure in a responsible way that doesn't include an escape from reality by way of some drug or another. Sex was created by God, but we have turned sexual activity into a dysfunctional escape from rather than a door into fidelity and godly pleasure.

It is indeed understandable that we would seek to take flight from pain. We often do not even realize that we are fleeing to our hiding places; we don't even know that they are hiding places. As I have seen in myself and the people around me, it takes courage to come out of hiding and face the life God would give us. If we do leave our hiding places, we find ourselves on a path that can require fortitude.

Fight

Some of us have personalities that are more inclined to *fight* pain than flee it. And, just as with flight, the fighting response can be positive. Many in the helping professions, for example, wage passionate war with pathology of various kinds. I am not suggesting that we abandon the fight against cancer or the social sins of our society or the psychological sicknesses that afflict so many people. There is a place for the fight against evil and its pain. But even in the Church, many of us are more intent on fighting off the pain that the devil inflicts than we are with absorbing the life that God can give. And if you ask anyone in law enforcement or the military they would say that a style of fighting can take over all of life.

Post-Traumatic Stress Disorder develops from defining life as a perpetual fight. This disorder is usually associated with soldiers returning from combat who have had a particularly traumatic experience. But people who are in law enforcement, child services, emergency medicine, social work, and even ministry can develop PTSD from constant exposure to intense and traumatizing pain. When the fight against the pain of evil comes to dominate a person, it can be difficult to leave the valley of battle. If the fight against pain becomes too pervasive, it can become difficult to enjoy family and friends and ordinary pleasures, or even to relax and rest.

THE PATHS

"How can I endure?" Does pain have the power to define us, to take over the meaning of our lives? If we are dominated by our *flight* from or our *fight* against pain, then the pain defines us. If we are dominated by the triumph of God's grace over all our pain, no matter how difficult, then we are on the path toward the heavenly places in Christ.

Three cairns stand out as markers of the trail forward: *repentance* of the pain we have caused, *forgiveness* of the pain life has caused us, and *transformation* of our experience of pain from life-threatening to life-giving.

Repentance

The cairn of *repentance* marks the beginning of the path toward answering the question, "How can I endure?" Repentance is usually associated with turning away from or changing our mind about sin. But repentance can also mean turning away from or changing our mind about a failed solution or a problem we have created.

God "repented" of the failed solution of making Saul king over Israel. It wasn't working out for Saul to be king, God said, "because he has turned away from me and has not carried out my instructions" (1 Sam. 15:11). You may recall that Israel had asked for an earthly king so they could be like other nations in Canaan (see 1 Samuel 8:5). But the success of that solution depended on the character and reliability of the king who was in authority. Saul's integrity left a lot to be desired, so God turned to David, "a man after his own heart" (1 Sam. 13:14). Obviously God was not repenting of sin; He was taking a different direction to solve Israel's leadership needs.

Flight or fight do not solve the problem of pain. When we see that the first cairn is repentance of taking the burden of pain on our own shoulders, we can begin to move forward on the upward path toward the heavenly places concerning our pain. We cannot move forward and pain cannot be transformed into the birth canal for newness of life until we release our efforts to solve the problem by flight or fight alone.

Forgiveness

Pain can leave you mad at life. I first learned this at a nursing home near a church I was serving. Local United Methodist ministers would go once each month to hold a church service and to visit with residents. During my orientation, the director had told me that many of the residents were "disappointed in life." But when I talked to the people myself, I did not see as much disappointment as I saw anger. My paternal grandfather was not a self-pitying or petulant man by any means, but he would sometimes sit on his porch swatting flies and when I would ask what he was thinking he would say, "'Tain't fair, son; 'tain't fair."

I once asked, "What isn't fair, granddad?"

He smiled and said, "Sometimes life isn't fair, son."

Life sometimes seems, indeed sometimes is, enormously unfair. Natural disasters, disease, abuse, financial hardship, other forms of what we colloquially call "hard times" can leave us angry—angry at life, angry at others who don't have the troubles we do, and angry at God. Is it wrong to be angry? Even David, the "man after [God's] own heart," felt this way:

> How long, Lord? Will you forget me forever?
>   How long will you hide your face from me?
> How long must I wrestle with my thoughts
>   And day after day have sorrow in my heart?
> How long will my enemy triumph over me? (Ps. 13:1–2)

Job is the classic biblical picture of anger at God's "unfairness." Job was a good man and so, of course, expected life to be good. That would only be fair, right? But then a series of medical, interpersonal, financial, and domestic losses made Job's life a swirling cauldron of pain. His friends scrutinized the details of his life and blamed his suffering on something he must have done wrong. Job's pain must be his fault. (The same voices arise today when a person is raped or robbed or ruined financially; the victim must have brought the situation on him- or herself.)

God visited with Job toward the end of the book. He did not give Job answers to his questions about why he was suffering. God simply gave Job himself. He showed Job who he was, and in revealing himself to Job, by entering into a relationship with Job in his pain, God led Job toward a forgiveness of life for being hard and painful at times. I wondered as a younger man why Job said, "I…repent in dust and ashes" (Job 42:6). Then experience with other people taught me. People modeled a healthy, Christian response to pain as they passed by the cairn of forgiveness, forgiving perpetrators of harm, forgiving "life," even forgiving God for allowing all that pain.

Forgiveness means that we can keep on loving others, life, and God in spite of painful circumstances. The word that is used in the grief literature such as Elisabeth Kübler-Ross's book, *On Death and Dying*, is "acceptance."[2] Either word—forgiveness or acceptance—can bring us past the primary cairn on the path toward an answer to our problem of pain.

Transformation

The experience of pain cannot be eliminated from our lives, but we can be *transformed* in the way we interpret pain. A person can interpret pain as a judgment of their lives or as a means to a fuller life. Joseph is one of the best examples of the transformation of pain into fullness of life. Nobody would enjoy being victim to human trafficking by one's own family, as Joseph was. But Joseph found resilience through forgiveness of his brothers who had sent him off to slavery, and he found himself in a position of power and influence in Egypt. When a famine threatened to annihilate his family in the land of Israel, the pain of Joseph's slavery positioned him to deliver his family, including the brothers who had sold him into slavery, from the pain of famine. Joseph's brothers cowered in fear when they realized that the brother they betrayed now had the power to destroy them. But instead of destroying his family, he said,

> Don't be afraid. Am I in the place of God? You intended to harm me, but God intended it for good to accomplish what is now being done, the saving of many lives. So then, don't be afraid. I will provide for you and your children. And he reassured them, and spoke kindly to them. (Gen. 50:19–21)

Pain that is surrendered to God can be transformed into life-giving circumstances just as surely as the pain of labor can bring forth the new life of a child. God's Spirit transforms pain into a womb out of which God brings new life.

There are several aspects of this transformation process, but three emerge as primary from the story of Joseph and throughout the Gospels: God's presence, power, and perspective. I mentioned earlier that during my liver transplant experience I kept hearing and repeating the same mantra, over and over: "I am with you; that is all you need" (2 Cor. 12:9, TLB).

When I conducted my first funeral back in 1978, I felt quite inadequate and didn't know how to help the mother whose son had been killed. The church lay leader said, in words that help me in ministry to this day, "Preacher, you are never going to know for sure how to help; but you can always give the help of your presence; just go put your hand on that mother's shoulder to let her know you're there." And I did. And she wept and told me later how much that pat on her shoulder gave her comfort in her pain.

The power of God does sometimes remove pain, but most often his power gives us the courage to endure and learn from our suffering. God's power is always directed strength. It is strength to do good; and the good comes back to strengthen us in our pain. Once not long before her death, during a Christmas visit, I asked my mother how she was doing. She was racked with the pain of the cancer she had fought for thirteen years. But she smiled a weak grin when I asked. She said, "Well I'm OK, I guess." She paused and added, "This can't keep me from praying for folks, though." I have her copy of *Living Light*.[3] It is filled with birthdays, anniversaries, and other significant events; on those days she would pray for those people. As God gave her the power to do good, that strength came back to her to help her endure to the end.

The perspective of God is not always available to us. He sees and knows and understands far more than we do, of course (see Isaiah 55:8ff). But he also gives us insight at times into what's going on in our lives. I wondered for many years why I had to go through the pain of alcoholism. Part of the reason, of course, is that my ministry would not have been what it is if not for the excruciating pain, devastating humiliation, and terror of addiction and recovery. But through some wonderful counselors, God helped me to understand he was using the disease of alcoholism to heal my life. I had been an incredibly arrogant young man, thinking I knew everything and was better than everybody. Through my painful experiences, God was healing me of that arrogance and was giving me the gift of perceiving the world through eyes of loving humility rather than disdainful arrogance. By walking through the pain, my heart was softened and changed.

THE HEAVENLY PLACES

If we endure, what is the outcome of our pain? It is one of the great paradoxes of life in Christ that the outcome of pain is *healing*, and the outcome of that healing is *celebration* of the life we have in the heavenly places in Christ Jesus. Pain borne alone can destroy life; pain transformed by God can give new life.

Healing

God always heals all our diseases (see Psalm 103:3). Sometimes he does so through removing a disease in ways that are beyond science to comprehend. Sometimes, often in fact, God heals through medicine. But sometimes, God heals us by using a disease to create a newness of life in us that would not have been there if not for the ongoing pain of illness.

The same is true for nonmedical experiences of suffering through which God gives us life. Think of the many painful experiences we have discussed in *Climbing Home*. God's Son is our Savior and Healer and he is "the way and the truth and the life" (John 14:6). The cross of Christ's intense suffering became under the mighty hand of God the instrument of our salvation, and that cross shows that God can use our own suffering to bring us into new life.

In accepting God's healing transformation, it is important that we learn to pray for that work in a biblical way. It is certainly biblical for us to pray for God to heal a medical, financial, marital, vocational, or other painful situation by removing the source of pain. But it is equally important to ask God for the courage, the wisdom, and the insight to experience his life-giving work *through* pain. It is important, in growing up into Christ in all things (see Ephesians 4:15), to let God be God. He is not an errand boy who will do our bidding if we just pray the right way. Let's pray for God's love to be manifested among us; it is up to God just what form that takes.

Celebration

We can be sure that if we allow God to work with us in his way and at his time, the outcome will be our *celebration* of the life of Christ within us and among us. The end result of Job's suffering was his restored life (see Job 42). The end result of Joseph's slavery was the survival of the family of Israel (see Genesis 50). The end result of my liver cancer was the gift of a transplant, renewed vigor, and the time to write *Climbing Home.*

But even when there are tragic ends to our suffering, we can still know the celebration of life that is ours in Christ. Oh, to be sure, there are times when the achievement of that celebration takes years of arduous psychological and spiritual work. But it's worth it. We can endure all the way through to celebration, struggling up the path past the cairns with unremitting faith in the God of the journey. We become one with Jesus in his crucifixion, and the pain inflicted by sin, by religion, by institutions, and by accidents enables us to celebrate with him our resurrection to newness of life.

THE QUESTIONS AND SCRIPTURES

1. What are the most painful experiences in your life and how have you dealt with them? How did those experiences leave you feeling toward God, toward yourself, toward others?
2. What have you gained from your most painful experiences? Are there people in your life who could benefit from your sharing those lessons?
3. What aspects of Christian faith and life have been most helpful to you in those sufferings? Are there claims of faith that have hindered rather than helped you?
4. If you were God, would you remove pain from the world? Why? What would Christian life look like without pain?
5. Is there someone—a minister, counselor, family member, or friend—you might need to consult? (Many ministers would be willing to help with referral to a counselor. You may need to be persistent, but it's worth it).
6. What is God trying to give you through the most painful aspect of your life right now? What do you need to do to receive what he wants to give you?
8. Scripture for further reflection: Gen. 45:1–8; 50:15–21; Job

1–3, 42; Ps. 13, 22, 42, 44; John 14–16; 2 Cor. 12:7–10; Eph. 6:10–17.

CHAPTER 15

DEATH: WHAT IS MY LIFE?

Very, very early morning is special. The stars, if the morning is clear, are radiant and, at mountain elevations of eleven or twelve thousand feet, they hang low to the ground, hovering and shimmering like a thousand diamonds suspended in the breath of God. There is an almost vocal quiet at that time, a silence in which you can hear soft whispers of Jesus, his Abba, and their Spirit in early-morning words of love. You can almost hear the quiet hum of their morning song floating on the breeze and settling on your ear like a dove landing from flight. In summer, a gentle dew caresses the earth with predawn moisture. Then, almost without notice at first, outlining the faces of a couple on a mountainside, a runner in the park, a child whose window faces east, or a stream wandering through a forest, the darkness ever so slowly recedes. Pale blues, then yellows, then oranges get painted by an unseen hand across the eastern horizon. Once the hills are outlined, smiles crease the faces that take in deep breaths of the morning air. The first light of day holds on its arm the striding sun, which marches steadily toward a new birth of the work of God. Life has begun again, with God.

Death in Christ, too, is a new day.

THE VALLEYS

We don't usually welcome death as we might a beautiful sunrise, of course. When we walk in "the valley of the shadow of death" (Ps. 23:4, NKJV), most of us are among those "who all their lives were held in slavery by their fear of death" (Heb. 2:15).

The psalmist sees death as a teacher of how to really live: "Teach us to number our days that we may gain a heart of wisdom" (Ps. 90:12). We can gain a deeper sense of life through awareness of death, but in order for that to happen we must first leave the valley of *denial* and *anger.* Both denial and anger can make death hold negative defining power over our lives.[1]

Denial

Irvin Yalom, in his book *Existential Psychotherapy*, provides a perceptive description of our *denial* of death.[2] That denial takes two forms: a belief in our own specialness or a belief in an ultimate rescuer. A narcissistic sense of our specialness can lead us to believe we will not die because we are so privileged that we will be granted an exemption from death, at least for a long time. You may think, "but that's not very rational." Yet how many times have you heard others say (or perhaps you have said it yourself), concerning a car wreck, heart attack, tornado, or other sudden appearance of death, "I just didn't think it would happen to me." Jesus speaks of the fool who tears down his barns to build bigger barns as if there's no tomorrow, saying to himself, "You have plenty of grain laid up for many years. Take life easy; eat, drink, and be merry." And Jesus warns, "You fool! This very night your life will be demanded of you" (Luke 12:19–20).

There is a more "Christian" denial of death that is both common and subtle: the belief that God will always prevent our death, that he will step in like a cosmic superman and rescue us at the last minute. This is an unbiblical belief just as it is unbiblical to claim that God will make all our diseases go away. He might do it sometimes, but he might not.

Jesus has not eliminated death but he has redefined it. When he said, "Everyone who lives and believes in me shall never die" (John 11:26, ESV), he did not mean that Lazarus did not die or would not die eventually again, but that through Christ death has been redefined as a transition. Death no longer has the last word. And in Christ, illness that may lead to death is not the last word. It is most definitely true that we are healed by Christ's stripes (see Isaiah 53:5) and that God "heals all your diseases" (Ps. 103:3). But he sometimes heals our lives *through* our diseases.

If that is what God is up to, then by his grace he may jolly well leave our diseases alone until we've gotten all the good that can come from them. That is the message of Paul concerning his thorn in the flesh (see 2 Corinthians 12:7); God used that problem, whatever it was, to create in Paul a dependence on God "that the power of Christ may rest on me" (2 Cor. 12:9). Rather than rescue us from death, God can use the reality of death to teach us and to bring us into conformity with Christ.

God does not promise that he will prevent our death; he does promise eternal life that triumphs over death. If we allow ourselves to twist Christian faith into a denial of death, we offend the work of the Spirit who teaches eternal life that conquers but most definitely goes through death. Denial of death is akin to replacing the biblical teaching of the resurrection of the body by a pagan belief in the immortality of the soul. We don't have eternal life because our souls are immortal; we have eternal life because "God raised us up with Christ and seated us with him in the heavenly realms in Christ Jesus" (Eph. 2:6). If we allow ourselves to be deceived into ascribing to God things that he has not promised, we can easily enter the other side of the valley of the shadow of death: *anger.*

Anger

Death can breed anger in us all, even among the people of God, perhaps especially in the people of God. When Jesus' friend, Lazarus, died in the Gospel of John, both Martha and Mary, Lazarus' sisters, were clearly perturbed that Jesus had delayed coming to their village until after their brother had died. They both said, "If you had been here, my brother would not have died" (John 11:21, 32). That is so very human, so very understandable. Namely, if God does his job, if he is there at the moment of death, surely he will keep death from happening.

But Lazarus' experience is our experience. We die. And when we die, Jesus, using the same love for us out of which he acted for Lazarus' sisters, will cut through our wall of anger. He will tear that wall down by his gracious promise of resurrection. After all, you can't have resurrection without death. Therefore, we need no longer to be angry at God for allowing death to be part of life.

Jesus is "the resurrection and the life" (John 11:25), "the way and the truth and the life" (John 14:6). Jesus says, "Because I live, you also will live" (John 14:19). He gives the ultimate promise, the one that leads out of the valley of the shadow of death with all of its denial and anger. Are you following him? Are you on the path to life?

THE PATHS

Gospel life triumphs over death. Resurrection is God breathing into the dry bones of our lives the breath of his new life.

The prophet Ezekiel saw a valley of dry bones that was like the dry, dead bones of our society today. And God said to Ezekiel:

> Son of man, these bones are the people of Israel. They say, "Our bones are dried up and our hope is gone; we are cut off." Therefore prophesy and say to them: "This is what the Sovereign Lord says: My people, I am going to open your graves and bring you up from them.... Then you, my people, will know that I am the Lord, when I open your graves and bring you up from them. I will put my Spirit in you and you will live...." (Ezek. 37:11–14)

Most of us, like the people of Israel, seek to triumph over death by trying to revise life. The gospel way is not a revision of the old way; it is the path of complete resurrection. Two cairns can help us stay on this path: *meaning* and *investment.* Each of these cairns represents a specific aspect of living in Christ as the way, the truth, and the life, as opposed to existing in a monotonous series of meaningless events with no future beyond the grave. If we are walking past these cairns on the path toward the heavenly places we are really living.

An illustration that has probably made the rounds of most preachers at one time or another goes like this: One night a little girl was saying her routine prayer before bed when she made a "mistake." She did not pray, "If I should die before I wake, I pray thee, Lord, my soul to take." She prayed instead, "If I should live before I die, I pray thee, Lord, my soul to make." When she apologized, embarrassed, for her goof, her mother gently and wisely said she had not made a mistake. That little girl and her mother knew that the real question about death is not about life after death but rather life before death.

Meaning

John Hus was one of the early rising stars of the Protestant Reformation who was influenced by John Wycliffe. He was burned at the stake for his faith. It is said that his last words were, "O sancta simplicitas" (O holy simplicity).[3] Although those words may have referred in jest to his executioners' difficulty in igniting the fire that killed him, they have been taken over as a watchword to mean ordinary, simple, unadorned life events that are experienced in Christ.

What does it mean to eat a meal, to earn a wage, to marry and have children, to create works of art, if the end of it all is death? That is the question of Ecclesiastes. The writer of that book anticipated some of the existentialist writings of the nineteenth and twentieth centuries who called into question the significance and meaning of life that is bound on one side by birth and on the other by death.

However, if life is experienced in Christ then all of existence can take on meaning. It has been a central theme of *Climbing Home* that all of the truth, the way, and the substance of life experienced in Christ can be filled with the purpose, the grace, the love, and the hope of the gospel of Christ. I would go even further to say that one of the greatest sins of Christian people in our day is a deficit of joy and an inability to grasp the meaning of life when it is carried out in trustful obedience to Jesus Christ.

Several years ago I was asked to conduct a workshop at a local church on household chores. The workshop was attended by about thirty married adult Christians who were earnestly seeking to grow in Christ. I asked at the beginning of the workshop how many of the participants had faith in Jesus Christ as their Lord and Savior. All raised their hands. I then asked how many of them had faith in Jesus Christ as the Lord and Savior of their housework. Most raised their hands, somewhat sheepishly, I might add. Then I asked how many of them thanked God the last time they experienced the pleasure of completing a good, hard day of house-cleaning. Many of the women raised their hands, but almost none of the men. After everyone chuckled at the discrepancy, I pointed out some research that found a statistically lower incidence of heart disease among men who do housework. I speculated those findings may correlate with the mindset and attitude of the men who do housework. Those who serve their wives and families in this way are like the Lord Jesus, who described himself "as one who serves" (Luke 22:27).

It is only when the meaning of the small, simple things becomes a part of our everyday experience of our Lord that we truly, truly "wake before we die." For this is just the beginning.

Investment

Because our life in Christ is just the beginning of eternal life, each moment is an investment. And it can be such an incredible joy to live life as an *investment* in the well-being of our fellow pilgrims on this earth. You may do something "spiritual" like teaching a Sunday school class, or you may change a tire, sell a loaf of bread, lead a political campaign, or wash a load of diapers. If our lives are lived with faith and hope and love, from dawn till dusk we invest in the building of the world as God made it to be. His first commandment still stands for Christian people; God commanded us to be "fruitful and increase in number, fill the earth and subdue it" (Gen. 1:28). It is the will of God that we live fully, live joyfully, and spend our lives helping others to do so as well. It is our privilege and responsibility in Christ to do life as an *investment* in the good life of the world around us. That includes any activity that is consistent with God's purpose for the fulfillment of human life, even cooking a pizza, preaching a sermon, trading stocks, feeding chickens, eating an apple, raising a family, teaching school, playing tennis, driving a cab, or reading a book.

God wants us to enjoy making an investment in the lives of our children and others who will come after us. The money you may bequeath to them is only part of it. My wife and I weren't real rich folks before her brain tumor and my liver cancer, but we were able to survive those expenses intact, for which we are quite grateful. After those events, let's just say we were even less materially rich than we were before. But we invest in our children, grandchildren, and others who will come after us in other ways. I was motivated to write *Climbing Home* as a legacy for our children, grandchildren, clients, students, church members, and friends. Has it been work? Has it been stressful? Just ask my wife! But oh, my goodness, has every word ever been rewarding; it's an investment in those I love (and in some readers I haven't even met).

My wife invests by crocheting. Not for money, but as an *investment* of love. She has made countless afghans, potholders, scarves, shawls, and all kinds of other things for our children, grandchildren, and friends. She knows that some of the gifts she has made are in a closet somewhere or tucked away because they don't match a bedspread or something, but you don't always get to see the return on an investment in your lifetime. And that's OK. This is just the beginning.

Our life in Christ is an investment in the pleasures at God's right hand not only on this earth but also in heaven. What we begin with God on this earth, God brings to completion in our life with him through all eternity. It is not, of course, that what we do with our life in Christ earns life in heaven; life in heaven is earned by Christ and Christ alone by his death and resurrection (see Ephesians 2:1–10). It is, however, a truth of the gospel that the life that is given as a gift of grace by Christ includes heaven, and the quality of our life in heaven can be enhanced by the quality of our life in Christ on this earth (see 1 Corinthians 4:1–5). Every meal we eat, every word we say, every act of hope, and faith, and love we carry out is an investment in the quality of life we will have in heaven.

Because this *is* the beginning.

THE HEAVENLY PLACES

What does it look like to live with death in the heavenly places, the mountains of hope, in our earthly journey? We have seen it does not mean we live in denial. We know that resurrection does not mean we will be rescued from the experience of death. A comedian was asked on his ninetieth birthday if he had reached any conclusions about his mortality. He quipped, "Indeed I have; I don't think any of us is going to get out of this alive."

Yet if we are alive in Christ, we do get out of this alive. Death becomes a transition like graduation, marriage, or retirement. Paul says that in light of the resurrection of Christ and our risen life in him we can "stand firm," always giving ourselves "fully to the work of the Lord, because you know that your labor in the Lord is not in vain" (1 Cor. 15:58). Seeing death as a transition will affect our journey, from this day forward, in two ways: we can *accept our increasing poverty* and we can *anticipate our coming wealth.*

Accept Increasing Poverty

Age may bring wealth financially. but it inevitably brings poverty of strength, mind, comfort, and time. There is no way to reconfigure the calendar in such a way as to have an equal amount of time remaining on this earth at seventy as we did at twenty. Acceptance of that reality is a good thing. Awareness of limited strength, comfort, mental ability, and time can teach a person to live as fully as possible, every day.

This is the message of one of the most beautiful passages in the Bible concerning the heavenly places of the people of God during a time of increasing poverty. During the time of Habakkuk, a period of poverty, of spirit, of material goods, and of homeland, was looming on the horizon. Babylonia was at the height of its power and there was a sense that they would soon conquer Israel. Nevertheless, the prophet wrote:

> Though the fig tree may not blossom,
> Nor fruit be on the vines;
> Though the labor of the olive may fail,
> And the fields yield no food;
> Though the flock be cut off from the fold,
> And there be no herd in the stalls—
> Yet I will rejoice in the Lord,
> I will joy in the God of my salvation.
> The Lord God is my strength;
> He will make my feet like deer's feet,
> And He will make me walk on my high hills. (Hab. 3:17–19, NKJV)

The prophet knew that a time of increasing poverty, akin to the increasing poverty of mind, comfort, strength, and time with the approach of death, can be a time of increasing praise in the heavenly places.

I have been grateful for my wife for so many reasons and for so many years. She remained by my side as I went through the very difficult years of recovery from alcoholism. She was not only willing but eager to go with me to beach, woods, and mountains to absorb the Word of God through the waves, trees, streams, rains, sun, and mountain vistas. She was willing to take her very Episcopalian spiritual identity into the backwoods of small United Methodist churches. She has been and is a wonderful mother and grandmother to our family. And there are other ways, which are private to her and me, in which I am so very grateful. We now lack the physical strength to climb a fourteen-thousand foot mountain, and we lack the strength to enjoy other pursuits of our younger years.

With our increasing poverty of mind and body and social life, I have begun praying a new prayer. Every single night, as we nestle into the gentle arms of sleep, I pray, "Dear Lord, I so thank you for giving me yet another day with this wonderful friend, playmate, and wife. Amen." Poverty of mind, strength, and time can give a new birth of gratitude for each new day, each new experience, each new gift of life.

Anticipation of Coming Wealth

When I was a little boy, the anticipation of what we called "vacation day" would build up for months. We might be going to north Alabama to visit my grandparents, to the beach in Panama City, Florida, or in later years to the woods for a Boy Scout camping trip. But for weeks my brother, sister, and I would wake up asking each other, "Is it the day yet?" Then we'd say, with all the exuberance of children living in hope of good times to come, "It's not the day, but it's on the way!"

That kind of joy can accompany the anticipation of good times to come after our commencement exercise ends our earthly journey. Life in that blessed hope can fill each of our remaining days with a joy and gladness. If we knew we were going to win the lottery, if we knew we were going to get to meet and have dinner with our favorite actor or baseball player or musician, if we had a certainty that we were going to be given title to a beautiful home in the mountains or on the beach, wouldn't that put a skip in our step and a smile on our lips? How much more if we lived in the certain knowledge that we were going to go on a mountain climb and that we would be able to sit and watch a sunrise with the one who created the first light of day!

Can you see it? Life in the heavenly places, reached through our coming death in Christ, can be fully lived now because of what life will be hereafter. The depression, the anxiety, the twisted distortions of pleasure and the agonizing avoidance of pain, all the dysfunction of sin and darkness that fills the valleys of the shadows of death, and all the ways we fail to live before we die, all evil and enemies of life—all of that will be disabled. Everything will meet its conqueror when the love of God in Christ Jesus our Lord comes.

> For he must reign until he has put all enemies under his feet. The last enemy to be destroyed is death. For he has put everything under his feet.... When he has done this, then the Son himself will be made subject to him who put everything under him, so that God may be all in all. (1 Cor. 15:25–28)

THE QUESTIONS AND SCRIPTURES

1. Who have you known who died with the most peace, confidence, and joy? What do you think gave them that serenity?
2. How does the reality of death affect your life (for example, "It makes me afraid to take risks," or "It makes me protective of my loved ones," or "I don't like to think about it")?
3. What do you wish you knew for sure about death? How could you achieve that assurance?
4. What are five areas in which the limitation of your days on this earth could help you live more fully (for example, time with your family, more time in devotions or exercise, date nights with your spouse)?
5. What would you like to do with Jesus 100 years from now? How does that thought affect you today?
6. What is preventing you from enjoying life here and now in the light of heaven then and there? What could you do about that obstacle?
7. What would God like to give you between now and the time of your death? What is on God's "bucket list" for you?
8. Scripture for further reflection: Ps. 90; Ezek. 37:1–14; John 11:1–44; 1 Cor. 15.

Conclusion

Mom began a new life on May 19, 2001. And what a life she had lived up to that day, when some would say she died. Those of us who knew her journey trusted that she was really very much alive, embarking on the next phase of the adventure of life. On the day of the funeral we stood in the first rows of the First United Methodist Church in Birmingham, Alabama surrounded by people of God, some still living on this earth and some part of a great cloud of witnesses who had gone on before us, and we sang. We sang of God a mighty fortress, a bulwark that never fails to provide a shield against all that would do us to death in our journey. We sang of all the saints surrounding us. We sang, oh how we all sang, choir and congregation, family and friends, living on this earth and standing with mom in the new levels of the heavenly places where she from her labors rested. Oh how we sang great hallelujahs to our King of Kings and our Lord of Lords. We embraced the passage of my mother to the eternal arms of the one she always simply called her Friend. The power of the love of Almighty God filled the room and our hearts and we could, if we listened closely, hear him whisper her new name and say to his child, "Welcome, welcome home to the heavenly places in which you began on this earth and in which you will live in deep glory, forever."

Mom was a follower.

Climbing Home has been a story of followers and of following. Mom came out of the bowels of her father's suicide to transform that tragedy, by following Jesus, into a wonderful new sense of the beauty and richness of life. I came out of the dungeon of alcoholism and the terror of cancer to emerge in a life of hope and peaceful confidence that in Christ life could be nothing but good. My wife broke out of the prison of codependency, having striven constantly and feverishly to find someone, somewhere, who would say she was loved and accepted without one plea or accomplishment. She also came out of the pain, the anxiety, the life-threatening proximity of a scalpel to discover a new call of God in her life. Others came out of poverty, promiscuity, depression, narcissism, rage, power, materialism, and more. All of us responded when we heard a voice saying, tenderly, softly, "Come home." We came out of many other valleys of deathly shadows and we followed.

We followed, sometimes fighting against the call with powerful resistance, out of the valleys that entrapped us in poisoned answers to our questions, in well-decorated prisons that masqueraded as satisfactions of our needs. We followed from one cairn to another, making our way toward a sunrise of life. We followed, and we are beginning, some of us, like Mom, to experience the land of promise, the heavenly places of play and pleasure that belong to our Friend and Lord.

We are a diverse group of followers, aren't we? And, you know, unity in diversity did not originate as a political fad but with Jesus Christ. Differences among the followers of Christ are inevitable, and yet, in his Son Jesus, the Father reconciles to himself "all things, whether on earth or in heaven, by making peace through the blood of his cross" (Col. 1:20). We follow differently, just as Ruth (great-grandmother of King David, Jesus' ancestor) came from Moabite tradition, her husband from Israelite tradition. Some, like John the one whom Jesus loved, follow closely. Some, like Saul of Tarsus, follow with resistance at first, then with tremendous ardor. Some, like James, follow behaviorally. Some, like the writer of Hebrews, follow historically and theologically. Some, like Peter, follow closely, then at a distance, denying their following. Then later, in repentance they follow as a leader of those who need extra strength to follow.

All, like Mom, follow a Savior, a Lord, a Friend who will never turn us away. Regardless of where we have been, regardless of the inconsistency of our following, regardless of our sin and waywardness, we keep following the One who always reaches out to bring us along the path.

We press onward—"...toward the goal for the prize of the upward call of God in Christ Jesus" (Phil. 3:14, NKJV).

It is a final witness of this book that it is not only OK, but it is also a mighty word of testimony to the grace of the one we follow that there is such diversity among the followers of Jesus. My own family of origin and my five sons are an example of this unity in diversity. Some of us follow conservatively, some liberally; some as Reformed, some as Methodist; some Catholic in denomination, and some catholic in spirit. Some of us are just beginning to leave the dark valleys of struggle. Some in my family, and I include myself, are already dwelling in the heavenly places. Some are focused on a single cairn of communion or music or stewardship or nature's wonders or a small Baptist church in the country. We are all following, although we are all at different stages and we express our faith differently. This diversity is not only OK but wonderful because it is a witness to the remarkable fact that it is not primarily we who follow Christ. It is, above all, Christ who follows us!

Wherever we go, Christ is seeking, following after us until He finds us (see Luke 19:10). He follows us to the last drop in the bottle of our addiction, and he is standing there knocking when we cry out of the bottom of our pain, "God, come for me." He follows us to the last dime we squeeze out of our employees until we cry out from the valley of our death through materialism, "God, come for me." He follows us to the hopeless end of our will to live when in one last desperate plea we cry out, "God, come for me." He follows us to the last breath of our loneliness when we feel that not only all people but all life has abandoned us, and he is standing there with the door held open when we cry out, "God, come for me."

He says, in the length and breadth and depth and height of his seeking us, following after us, "Look! Look at the manger. Look at the cross. Look at the empty tomb. Look at the sunrise this morning. Look at the smile on that face, and the hope in that child. Look into the communion glass, and look at the broken bread. Look at that mountain, that stream, and that church pew waiting for you. Look at your mother who followed. Look at your own heart crying for me to come to you"

Let's look at all the Words of God all around and within us. Let's follow the one who followed his Father's love into the humiliation of the cross, who followed us into all our dark valleys, who follows the path forward and then lays us gently down in the green pastures of the heavenly places. Let's follow Jesus "…the author and finisher of our faith, who for the joy that was set before him endured the cross, despising the shame, and has sat down at the right hand of the throne of God" (Heb. 12:2, NKJV).

"I am coming to you," he says (John 14:19). And, as we finish *Climbing Home,* he looks into our eyes as we seek the path to life and says, simply, powerfully, "Follow me" (John 21:21).

Appendix A

Letter concerning diagnosis of cancer (FAQs concerning practical arrangements omitted):

August 15, 2010, 10th Sunday after Pentecost

Dear Family, Friends, Colleagues, and Clients:

I wanted to share with you an opportunity that has been given to Calder, to me, and to you as well. And I wanted to share this opportunity in a letter for clarity of communication and to circumvent the fuzzy thoughts/words of the infamous "grapevine." This opportunity is yours as well as ours because we are all connected, some by blood, some by time together in various gardens and trenches, all as objects of God's love and grace in Jesus Christ, and hopefully all as growing recipients of that love and grace. Hopefully, we also increasingly share the perception that life is good, without exception, when life gets done in that love and grace. This letter invites you to, with us, further stretch that perception of life as good to include times of occasional severe difficulty, to include what some would call "bad times."

I have been diagnosed with liver cancer secondary to my Hepatitis C and, after passing a few more tests, which I'm told shouldn't be a problem, will be on the list at UT Southwestern Medical Center for a liver transplant. My diagnosis should place me on the list for transplant in 3–5 months. The outcomes for liver transplant are quite positive: 88% survive after 1 year, 81% after 3 years. And of course these numbers can be lifted higher by lifestyle, medical compliance, spiritual and support resources, and positive perception of the process.

But those numbers don't tell the whole story, as your various numbers don't tell the whole story of your lives. As we had believed before, and came to experience at a new level in relation to Calder's brain surgery last October, Christ casts none of us out. In Him there is 100% survival. Much of that can begin, if we let it, on this earth; the rest awaits an unbroken circle, a day crowning the King of kings in a place of quiet rest the Thomases rejoiced to glimpse in a service celebrating the home-going of our father on a late July day in 2002. In Christ, who says, "…the one who lives and believes in me shall never die" (John 11). So, we invite you to experience with us the good to come, not knowing what the good will look like.

Now, to anticipate a probable question.

Isn't all this good-in-difficulty stuff New Age gobbledygook at best, denial of pain at worst? I answer with a story.

We left at 1:47 AM, Sept. 17, 1999, 5 days shy of 9 months after my left hip surgery on Dec. 22, 1998. We were tired but exhilarated, pumped with an infusion of the quiet energy of grace. It was our third attempt. And it started quietly, leaving the car at 2:30 AM and walking about 2½ hours in soft darkness, except for our headlamps, toward a mysteriously gorgeous emergence of the sky's praise of God in the first, oh so dim, light of day, then the brilliance of sunrise above timberline. We continued on about an hour on a pretty good climber's trail. Then the trail became an intermittent series of smooth spots interspersed with footstool- to sofa-sized talus and boulders. It was along this stretch that it happened; the thing climbers with artificial hips fear. I fell. A hard fall. My left forearm and the palm of my right hand felt the blow of my full weight against sharp, unrelenting granite. I lay there catching my breath, then saying, "I'm OK, I'm OK, I'm OK" to quiet Calder's yelps. After we determined that nothing was broken, we talked.

It would have been so, so easy to quit; we'd seen an incredible sunrise; we were quite tired; I was buggered up. But it was September. First snows had freckled the granite as we climbed, and this was likely the last attempt of this year. And I had jolted myself out of depression on a hospital bed on Dec. 25, 1998 with the thought that I would climb a fourtee-thousand foot mountain within 12 months; and on that hospital bed I had begun to wiggle my feet as my first exercise toward this day. It would be OK not to summit; it was not OK not to try. And so we continued.

We continued over increasingly difficult talus, 8 hours on the stuff including descent; we continued through more snow; we continued beyond tired. We continued on a grueling, step-by-step, hour-after-plodding-hour ordeal. It was, to quote one climber's guidebook, "unpleasant."

But once in a while we stopped. We shifted perspective from the next boulder to the Arkansas River valley stretching out further and further to the east; we shifted focus to the surrounding summits growing nearer and nearer. We stopped to take a picture or two, knowing that what was going on here was much bigger than the pain we increasingly felt in parts of our bodies we didn't know had been there. And then we kept on. And on. And on. And on. And on. And on.

And we got back to the car at 8:53 PM, about 18 hours after we had started to climb. It had been hard, difficult, painful and we were inexpressibly exhausted.

But God had infused his grace, the grace given in Jesus Christ, into us through the whole process.

And so we summited Princeton.

And it was good.

And it was not gobbledygook-good, or denial-of-pain good. It was the "very good" that comes from God to all sorts and conditions of humankind when he breathes into their otherwise meaninglessly painful existences the breath of his saving new creation. It was the "very good" of creation restored. And it was the "very good" that transcends pain to give all life meaning, and joy, and hope.

And we invite you to join us in expecting and experiencing, without prior definition of what the good will look like, the good that will come from God's infusing his grace through surgeons and nurses and medicines and a donor's liver and support and innumerable steps into this cancer. We invite you to walk with us toward this summit.

In gratitude,
Madoc

Appendix B

Devotional for April 10 from *Daily Light on the Daily Path:*[1]

April 10 Morning

I am dark, but lovely.

Behold, I was brought forth in iniquity, and in sin my mother conceived me. *"Your fame went out among the nations because of your beauty, for it was perfect through My splendor which I had bestowed on you," says the Lord God.

I am a sinful man, O Lord!* Behold, you are fair, my love! Behold, you are fair!

"I abhor myself, and repent in dust and ashes." * You are all fair my love, and there is no spot in you.

I find then a law, that evil is present with me, the one who wills to do good.* Be of good cheer; your sins are forgiven you.

I know that in me (that is in my flesh) nothing good dwells.* You are complete in Him.* Perfect in Christ Jesus.

You were washed,... You were sanctified,...you were justified in the name of the Lord Jesus and by the Spirit of our God.* That you may proclaim the praises of Him who called you out of darkness into His marvelous light.

Song of Sol. 1:5; Ps. 51:5; Ezek. 16:14; Luke 5:8; Song of Sol. 4:1; Job 42:6; Song of Sol. 4:7; Rom.7:21; Matt. 9:2; Rom 7:18; Col 2:10; Col 1:28; I Cor. 6:11; I Pet. 2:9

Endnotes

Introduction

1. Phillips Brooks, *O Little Town of Bethlehem* (1868) taken from the United Methodist Hymnal 4th edition (Nashville: United Methodist Publishing House), #240.

Chapter 1: TRUTH: Whom can I trust?

1. James W. Fowler, *Stages of Faith: The Psychology of Human Development and the Quest for Meaning (*New York: Harper One, 1995). First published 1981 by Harper Collins.
2. Bartlett, John, *Familiar Quotations: A Collection of Passages, Phrases, and Proverbs Traced to their Sources in Ancient and Modern Literature,* 14th ed., Edited by Emily Morison Beck (Boston: Little, Brown, and Company, 1968), 261.
3. Ibid., 286.
4. Anne Graham Lotz, *Daily Light for Every Day* (Nashville: J. Countryman, a division of Thomas Nelson, Inc., 1998), First published in 1794 in Great Britain by Samuel Bagster.
5. Harriett Olson, et al., eds., *The Book of Discipline of the United Methodist Church 2000* (Nashville: United Methodist Publishing House, 2000), 77.

Chapter 2: HOME: Where do I belong?

1. *Original Sacred Harp,* (Denson Revision), T. J. Denson and S.M Denson and others, editors. (Haleyville, Ala.: Sacred Harp Publishing Company, Inc., 1936).
2. Robert Frost, *The Poetry of Robert Frost: The Collected Poems, Complete and Unabridged,* ed, Edward Connery Lathem, 1st ed. (New York: Holt, Rinehart and Winston, 1979), 1st published 1916, 257.
3. Thomas Hardy, *The Life and Death of The Mayor of Casterbridge: A Story of A Man of Character* (New York: Signet: New American Library,1962).

4. Ibid., 327.
5. *A River Runs Through It.* Dir. by Robert Redford, Columbia Pictures,1999.
6. Frank B. Minirth, *Happiness Is a Lifestyle: Choosing to Make a Positive Change,* (Grand Rapids, Mich.: Revell, 2005).

CHAPTER 3: IDENTITY: WHO AM I?

1. Brennan Manning, *Abba's Child: The Cry of the Heart for Intimate Belonging* (Colorado Springs, Colo.: Navpress, 1994).
2. Bernard J. Tyrrell, *Christotherapy: Healing through Enlightenment* (New York: The Seabury Press, 1975).

CHAPTER 4: PURPOSE: WHY AM I HERE?

1. Hannah Whithall Smith, *The Christian's Secret of a Happy Life* (Grand Rapids, Mich.: Revell, 2012). First printed 1952.
2. Thornton Wilder, *Our Town: A Play in Three Acts.* (New York: Perennial Library, 1985). Reprinted by arrangement with the Estate of Thornton Wilder. Original published 1938 by Harper & Row.
3. Ibid., 99.
4. Gregory Bateson, Stewart Brand, ed., *Steps to an Ecology of Mind: A Revolutionary Approach to Man's Understanding of Himself.* 13th ed. (New York: Ballantine Books, 1985). Original copyright 1972 Chandler Publishing.
5. Rick Warren, *The Purpose Driven Life: What on Earth Am I Here For?*(Grand Rapids, Mich.: Zondervan, 2002).
6. Oswald Chambers, *My Utmost for His Highest,* "Faith or Experience" (devotion for November 10, 2013), http://utmost.org/faith-or-experience (accessed March 20, 2014).

CHAPTER 5: GRACE: HOW CAN I LIVE FULLY?

1. Bartlett, op. cit., 750.
2. Lloyd John Ogilvie, *Autobiography of God: God Revealed in the Parables of Jesus,* (Ventura, Calif.: Regal Books, 1981).
3. Robert Boyd Munger, *My Heart Christ's Home,* 2nd rev. ed. (Downers Grove, Ill.: InterVarsity Press).

4. Rob Wylanda, *The 17:18 Series: Psalms 1–72, Psalms 73–150,* (Grand Rapids, Mich.: Reformation Heritage Books, 2010).
5. Lloyd John Ogilivie, *God's Will in Your Life,* (Eugene, Ore.: Harvest House, 1982).

PART II: QUESTIONS OF LOVE

1. Karl Barth, *Church Dogmatics: The Doctrine of Creation, Volume III, Part One,* ed. G. W. Bromily and T. F. Torrance, trans. J. W. Edwards and others, (Edinburgh: T & T Clark, 1958), 182–205.

CHAPTER 6: LOVE: WILL I BE ALONE?

1. Debra Fileta, *True Love Dates: Your Indispensable Guide to Finding the Love of Your Life* (Grand Rapids, Mich.: Zondervan, 2013).
2. Henry Cloud and John Townsend, *Boundaries: When to Say Yes, How to Say No, to Take Control of Your Life* (Grand Rapids, Mich.: Zondervan, 2002).
3. Anne Graham Lotz, op cit.
4. Debra Fileta, op cit.
5. Prayer of St. Chrysostom taken from *The Episcopal Book of Common Prayer* (Greenwich, Conn.: The Seabury Press, 1952), 20.
6. Philip D. Yancey, *Church: Why Bother?* (Grand Rapids, Mich.: Zondervan, 1998).

CHAPTER 7: CHOICES: WHO COMES FIRST?

1. P. Watzlawick, J. H. Weakland, and R. Fisch, *Change: Principles of Problem Formation and Problem Resolution* (New York: W. H. Norton, 1974).
2. Karl Barth, *The Epistle to the Romans,* 6th ed., trans. Edwyn C. Hoskyns (London: Oxford University Press, 1933).
3. Karl Barth, *Final Testimonies,* ed. Eberhard Busch, trans. by Geoffrey W. Bromiley (Grand Rapids, Mich.: William B. Eerdmans, 1977), 29–30.

CHAPTER 8: VALUE: WHAT IS WORTHWHILE?

1. E. Madoc Thomas, *Values, Therapeutic Alliance, and Marital*

Therapy: A Study of the Therapist-Client Relationship in Marital Therapy, Doctor of Philosophy Dissertation, Texas Tech University, 1994.
2. James I. Robertson, Jr. *Stonewall Jackson: the Man, the Soldier, the Legend.* (New York: Macmillan Publishing USA, 1997).
3. Karl Menninger and Martin Mayman and Paul Pruyser, *The Vital Balance: The Life Process in Mental Health and Illness*, (New York: Viking Press, 1963). Reprint by Penguin Books 1979.
4. M. Scott Peck, *The Road Less Travelled.* (London: Arrow Books, 2006). First published 1978 by Random House.
5. Grant Wood, *American Gothic* (painting), (Art Institute of Chicago, 1930).
6. Catherine Marshall, *A Man called Peter: The Story of Peter Marshall.* 4th printing (Grand Rapids, Mich.: Baker Books, 2006). First printing 1951.

CHAPTER 9: CALLING: WHAT CAN I GIVE?

1. Os Guinness, *The Call: Finding and Fulfilling the Central Purpose of Your Life* (Nashville: W Publishing, 2003).
2. Bob Goff, *Love Does: Discover a Secretly Incredible Life in an Ordinary World* (Nashville: Thomas Nelson, 2012).
3. John Ed Mathison, *Every Member in Ministry* (Nashville: Discipleship Resources, 1992).
4. Os Guinness, op cit., 119–122.

CHAPTER 10: PEACE: WILL I BE OK?

1. National Weather Service Forecast Office, Huntsville, Alabama, *NWS Huntsville 1974 Tornadoes,* http:www.srh.noaa.gov (accessed Mar. 15, 2014).
2. Christopher Madoc Thomas, "All Things Work for Good: The Rise and Fall of the Confederacy in the Southern Presbyterian Ministry" (unpublished Master's thesis, Texas Tech University, 2003), 3.

PART III: QUESTIONS OF HOPE

1. Bartlett, op. cit. 408.

CHAPTER 11: HOPE: WHAT CAN I EXPECT?

1. *Alcoholics Anonymous: The Story of How Many Thousands of Men and Women Have Recovered from Alcoholism,* 3rd ed. (New York: Alcoholics Anonymous World Services, 1976), 30–32.
2. For example, Brother Lawrence, *The Practice of the Presence of God,* (Grand Rapids, Mich.: Baker Books, 1989).
3. Karen Horney, *Self-Analysis*, (New York: W.W. Norton & Co., 1942).
4. Albert Outler, ed., *John Wesley* (New York: Oxford University Press, 1964), 272–282.
5. Westminster Confession, Question 1 ("Q. 1. What is the chief end of man? A. Man's chief end is to glorify God, and to enjoy him for ever.").
6. Brooks, "O Little Town of Bethlehem," op. cit.
7. William Glasser, *Schools Without Failure*, (New York: Perennial Library Harper & Row, 1975).

CHAPTER 12: RESOURCES: WILL I HAVE ENOUGH?

1. Albert Outler, op cit., 247–249.
2. Abraham H. Maslow, *Motivation and Personality,* 2nd ed. (New York: Harper & Row, 1970).
3. William F. Harley, Jr., *His Needs Her Needs: Building an Affair-Proof Marriage* (Grand Rapids, Mich.: Baker Books, 2003).
4. Richard Foster, *Freedom of Simplicity: Finding Harmony in a Complex World* (New York: HarperCollins, 1981, 1998).
5. John Eldredge, *Wild at Heart: Discovering the Secret of a Man's Soul* (Nashville: Thomas Nelson, 2001).
6. John Eldredge and Staci Eldredge, *Captivating: Unveiling the Mystery of a Woman's Soul* (Nashville: Thomas Nelson, 2005).

CHAPTER 13: PLEASURE: HOW CAN I ENJOY LIFE?

1. Saint Augustine, *The Confessions: Saint Augustine of Hippo* (Ignatius Critical Editions), ed. Fr. David Meconi, trans. Sr. Maria Boulding, O.S.B., (Hyde Park, NY: New York City Press, 1997 by the Augustinian Heritage Institute, Villanova, PA).

2. John Piper, *Desiring God.* 3rd ed., (Sisters, Ore.: Multnomah, 2003).

3. Clifford and Joyce Penner, *The Gift of Sex: A Guide to Sexual Fulfillment* (Waco, Tex: Word Publishing, 1981).

4. Judith K. and Jack O. Balswick, *Authentic Human Sexuality: An Integrated Christian Approach.* 2nd ed. (Downers Grove, Ill.: InterVarsity Press, 2008).

5. M. Scott Peck, op cit., 6–9.

6. David Elkind, *The Hurried Child: Growing Up too Fast Too Soon*, 3rd ed. (Cambridge, Mass.: Perseus Publishing, 2001). First published 1981.

7. *Places in the Heart*, directed by Robert Benton.

8. From the hymn, "O for a Thousand Tongues to Sing," Charles Wesley, 1739.

CHAPTER 14: PAIN: HOW CAN I ENDURE?

1. Oscar Cullmann, *Christ and Time: The Primitive Conception of Time* (Westminister, Colo.: Westminster Publishers, 1950).

2. Elisabeth Kübler-Ross, MD, *On Death and Dying* (New York: Simon & Schuster, 1997),123–146.

3. Edythe Draper, *Living Light, Daily Light* in today's language (Wheaton, Ill.: Tyndale House Publishers, 1972).

CHAPTER 15: DEATH: WHAT IS MY LIFE?

1. These are recognized as two of the stages of grief as developed by Elisabeth Kübler-Ross in her classic book, *On Death and Dying*, op cit., 51–93.

2. Irvin D. Yalom, *Existential Psychotherapy* (New York: Basic Books, Yalom Family Trust, 1980), 117–140.

3. William R.Cannon,. *History of Christianity in the Middle Ages: From the fall of Rome to the fall of Constantinople* (Nashville: Abington, 1960), 307–310.

APPENDIX B

1. Anne Graham Lotz, op cit., April 10.

NOTES